1. PIZ BERNINA 4049 m
2. LAUTERAARHORN 4042 m
3. SCHRECKHORN 4078 m
4. FINSTERAARHORN 4274 m
5. GROSS GRÜNHORN 4044 m
6. HINTERES FIESCHERHORN 4025 m
7. GROSSES FIESCHERHORN 4049 m
8. MÖNCH 4107 m
9. JUNGFRAU 4158 m
10. ALETSCHHORN 4193 m
11. LAGGINHORN 4010 m
12. WEISSMIES 4017 m
13. DÜRRENHORN 4035 m
14. HOHBERGHORN 4219 m
15. STECKNADELHORN 4241 m
16. NADELHORN 4327 m
17. LENZSPITZE 4294 m
18. DOM 4545 m
19. TÄSCHHORN 4491 m
20. ALPHUBEL 4206 m
21. ALLALINHORN 4027 m
22. RIMPFISCHHORN 4199 m
23. STRAHLHORN 4190 m
24. NORDEND 4609 m
25. DUFOURSPITZE 4634 m
26. ZUMSTEINSPITZE 4563 m
27. SIGNALKUPPE 4554 m
28. PARROTSPITZE 4432 m
29. LUDWIGSHÖHE 4341 m
30. SCHWARZHORN 4322 m
31. VINCENT PYRAMID 4215 m
32. PUNTA GIORDANI 4046 m
33. EASTERN LYSKAMM 4527 m
34. WESTERN LYSKAMM 4479 m
35. CASTOR 4223 m
36. POLLUX 4092 m
37. ROCCIA NERA 4075 m
38. BREITHORN 4106 m
39. EASTERN BREITHORN 4139 m
40. CENTRAL BREITHORN 4159 m
41. WESTERN BREITHORN 4164 m
42. MATTERHORN 4478 m

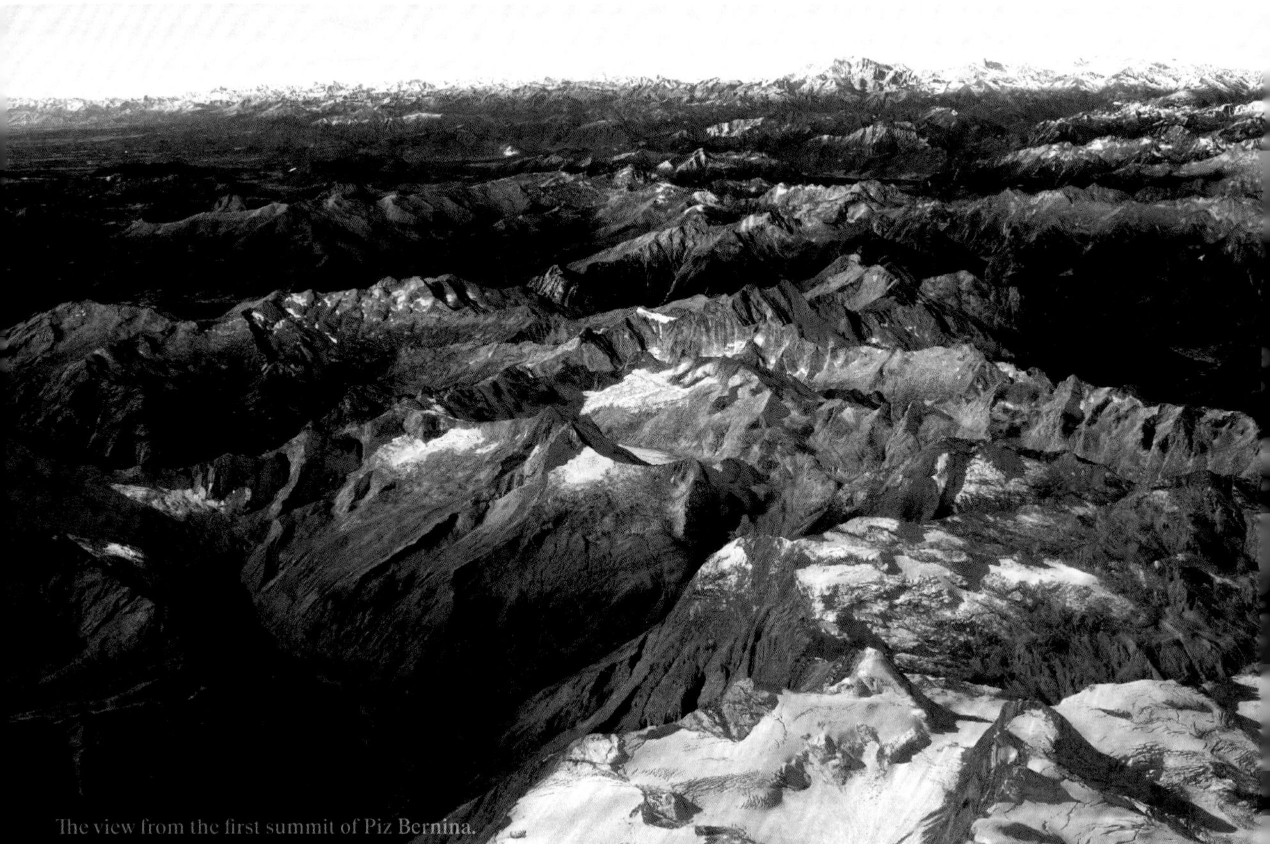
The view from the first summit of Piz Bernina.

43.	DENT D'HÉRENS	4171 m
44.	DENT BLANCHE	4357 m
45.	OBER GABELHORN	4063 m
46.	ZINALROTHORN	4221 m
47.	WEISSHORN	4505 m
48.	BISHORN	4153 m
49.	COMBIN DE VALSOREY	4184 m
50.	COMBIN DE GRAFENEIRE	4314 m
51.	COMBIN DE LA TSESSETTE	4135 m
52.	POINTE WALKER	4208 m
53.	POINTE WHYMPER	4184 m
54.	POINTE CROZ	4110 m
55.	POINTE ELENA	4045 m
56.	POINTE MARGUERITE	4065 m
57.	DÔME DE ROCHEFORT	4015 m
58.	AIGUILLE DE ROCHEFORT	4001 m
59.	DENT DU GÉANT	4013 m
60.	AIGUILLE VERTE	4122 m
61.	GRANDE ROCHEUSE	4102 m
62.	AIGUILLE DU JARDIN	4035 m
63.	LES DROITES	4000 m
64.	CORNE DU DIABLE	4064 m
65.	POINTE CHAUBERT	4074 m
66.	POINTE MÉDIANE	4097 m
67.	POINTE CARMEN	4109 m
68.	L'ISOLÉE	4114 m
69.	MONT BLANC DU TACUL	4248 m
70.	MONT MAUDIT	4465 m
71.	MONT BLANC	4809 m
72.	DÔME DU GOÛTER	4304 m
73.	AIGUILLE DE BIONNASSAY	4052 m
74.	MONT BLANC DE COURMAYEUR	4748 m
75.	PIC LUIGI AMEDEO	4469 m
76.	MONT BROUILLARD	4069 m
77.	PUNTA BARETTI	4013 m
78.	GRAND PILIER D'ANGLE	4243 m
79.	AIGUILLE BLANCHE DE PEUTEREY	4112 m
80.	GRAN PARADISO	4061 m
81.	BARRE DES ÉCRINS	4102 m
82.	DÔME DE NEIGE	4015 m

The data on summit elevations come from the International Climbing and Mountaineering Federation. www.theuiaa.org/4000-alps/

A NEW CHALLENGE

5

My experience in the Alps was transformational. The long days spent in the mountains over the years, and the hours of solitude and reflection they bring, have helped me discover who I truly am deep down. I am now beginning to understand my motivations, my fears and also my limits with a growing sense of certainty.

As I didn't want my memory to play tricks on me nor for time to slowly fade some of my footprints, I wanted to write about my journey across eighty-two different 4,000-metre (13,123-feet) peaks in the Alps, something I call my *Alpine Connections* project, or more affectionately, my *Petite balade alpine*. I have learned many things, and I'm still taking them all in. Perhaps sharing them can be useful to other people.

I was born in the Pyrenees in 1987, and I lived in my beloved Cap del Rec mountain shelter right up until I was nearly a teenager. That's where I took my first steps upwards, seeking elevation gain, starting with the Tossa Plana de Lles when I was only three years old. With my parents, we climbed 3,000-metre (9,850-feet) summits. When I was eleven, along with my sister, who's only a year apart from me, we walked across the Pyrenees from the Mediterranean all the way to the Atlantic in forty-two days. This is where I come from.

I've spent a lot of time in these mountains. Later, I settled in Chamonix in the Alps, and more recently in Norway. But deep down, I'm a child of the Pyrenees. Over the years of trekking up and down, I felt that I needed to return to the scents, the texture of the rocks, and the environment. I needed to rediscover the summits of my homeland. I wanted to do so in an ethical and aesthetic manner, and at the same time make the project a physical and mental challenge. That is what motivated me to cross the Pyrenees by linking the main 3,000-metre (9,850-feet) peaks. I wanted return to trekking on the mountains, at a steady, fluid pace – finding unexpected delights and thrills along the way – and to decide on the fly which trail to take, especially if I encountered a magnificent peak I wanted to climb. I did just that, in October 2023, over 155 hours of physical activity, covering 485 kilometres (300 miles) and doing 43,000 metres (14,000 feet) of ascent. It was an incredible experiment, a genuine rite of passage.

What I saw there captivated me so much that I wanted to continue exploring not only the mountain but who I was at my core. The idea of a new challenge started to take shape. Back home in Norway, it didn't take too much to imagine what I wanted to try out next. Four letters summarized my next goal: Alps.

↑ 10.10.23/SUMMIT OF PICA D'ESTATS
The moment I completed the Pyrenees project after finishing the traverse. I hugged my mother, remembering all the moments spent on these summits that have shaped who I am.

← P. 4
07.10.23/PYRENEES
I have always wanted to explore the mountains in a fast and lightweight manner. In 2023 I linked all the peaks over 3,000 metres (9,850 feet) in the Pyrenees in eight days, starting at Frondella and ending at Pica d'Estats.

↑ 04.10.23/PYRENEES
The traverse of the most iconic peaks in the Pyrenees was demanding. Yet, despite the sheer exhaustion, reaching the top of every mountain made it all worthwhile. I managed to cross over forty peaks in a single 'day' (stage), walking for thirty-nine hours straight and linking certain sections with my bike.

I was quite familiar with the Alps after having lived there for a decade. In the past I had dreamed about the possibility of creating long traverses across different ranges. So in a way, the idea of undertaking a great journey that links the most iconic peaks of the Alps had already been brewing in my mind, even if I wasn't fully aware of it.

My sources of inspiration were very clear: the vision of Patrick Berhault, the first traverse across the four-thousanders completed by Martin Moran and Simon Jenkins, the journey by Franz Nicolini and Diego Giovannini (who did it in sixty days in 2008), along with the one by Ueli Steck (in sixty-two days in 2015). Their milestones all gave me enormous motivation, because if they all had the same principle in common: they didn't want to compromise the integrity of the experience. They weren't seeking to beat records, but rather to explore the terrain. We all wanted to accomplish the feat without using any motor vehicles, without chasing performance at any price.

I had read all that I could about Berhault's project. I delved into Moran and Nicolini's books, and I had followed Ueli during

his traverses. Even if I shared the same goal with them, the legendary ascent of eighty-two four-thousanders powered only with human effort, I wanted to do it in a way that it was more like a long 'seamless' traverse than a series of multiple interlinked ascents.

I wanted to design the project as a comprehensive, coherent route that followed the natural line of the mountains, shunning the idea of linking ascents as if they were isolated milestones. Based on maps, route descriptions and conversations with mountaineering friends, I designed what I thought was the most logical and aesthetically pleasing route possible: a succession of ridges and lines that connected the summits following a physically and visually coherent strategy. The goal was to always stay within the massifs, moving forward without descending to the bottom of any valley, and resting only in mountain huts or preparing a bivouac when necessary, until each traverse was completed. Only then would I descend to access the following ridge and continue the journey.

But my plan wasn't entirely successful and I faced a few hurdles along the way. Sometimes the terrain wasn't how I had

↑ **11.06.13 / MONT BLANC**
Exploring mountains with a strong, well thought-out style. But this was nothing new: I had already undertaken the *Summits of My Life* project back in 2012, during which I climbed mountains around the globe.

↑ 21.08.13 / MATTERHORN
The *Summits of My Life* project brought me to the Alps, where I completed three great ascents and traverses: Courmayeur–Chamonix via the Innominata, the ascent of Mont Blanc from Chamonix and probably the one that impressed me most: the ascent of the Matterhorn from Cervinia in 2 hours and 52 minutes.

expected; other times the weather was problematic. As we all know: nature always wins!

My main focus when designing the route was that it was aesthetically pleasing. I started by sketching out the routes along the ranges I knew best: MONT BLANC and Valais. Then came the ranges with isolated peaks: BERNINA, WEISSMIES and GRAND COMBIN, which I had never explored, and GRAN PARADISO and ÉCRINS, which I had already traversed. To cap it off, I would finish with another great range that I had never stepped foot on, the Bernese Alps.

I planned a route that I deemed feasible and contacted friends, and friends of friends, to ask their opinions about parts of the trail that I had mapped out. In total, there were more than 150 climbing routes to try. Some would be tough, with sections with hardly any information at all; others would be more doable, while there were a few that I wasn't sure whether I'd make or not until I was there. Everything would depend greatly on the weather, on how I felt and, unfortunately, on the conditions caused by climate change, which has led to profound transformations in routes that I had considered a few years earlier.

‘A mountain lover dreams of conquering peak after peak, spending their life moving forward, ascending, descending, repeating, enduring pain and finding joy in it: this is the very essence of Kilian Jornet’s life. He pursues a form of knowledge that goes beyond sport; he is laying the ethical and physiological foundations for the future of mountaineering.’

ÓSCAR GOGORZA

Óscar Gogorza is a journalist specializing in mountain sports and climbing. He has been writing for *El País* since 1998 and runs the blog ‘El Montañista’. He is also an IFMGA-accredited high-mountain guide and the author of the book *Montaña*.

Even if I had a plan with an ideal route and the itineraries perfectly planned, I needed to be prepared for changes. Numerous alterations might require me to improvise and find solutions or alternative routes, places to stop or different techniques to continue when the weather or the conditions on the ground were not the ones that I had expected at the start.

In the summer of 2024, my family and I were already thinking about travelling to the Alps to race the Sierre-Zinal, a competition that has meant so much to my career. I thought that it would be a good idea to start the *Alpine Connections* project right after finishing this race. And so, as soon as the weather forecast seemed decent enough, off we went! I believed – and I'm still convinced, even though I didn't actually achieve it – that, with the perfect conditions, it's possible to traverse all the peaks in two weeks.

Starting my mission in mid-August had certain advantages, but also a few drawbacks. On the plus side, the glaciers at this time of year are quite dry, which means that the crevices are visible and therefore there is less risk of falling in them and also of snow bridges breaking. The lack of snow on the rocky crests also makes it possible to progress more quickly. On the other hand, the dryness means that the crevasses are more difficult to cross while the rocks on the walls are more unstable – making the trail all the more dangerous.

It's clear that a journey like this is not only about physical ability, but also very much about the people around you. This project is as much mine as it belongs to all those who have helped along the way. It was incredible sharing sections of the journey with old friends, while also making new ones. I spent time with amazing people like Philipp, Mathéo, Genís, Noa, Michel, Bastien, Jordi, Jules, Leo, Emily and Benjamin. I always received a warm welcome at the mountain huts, and am very

↑ 12.08.24 / SAINT-MORITZ
I brief the film crew on the entire route and how I plan to organize the logistics. The day before the traverse began, the team was faced with a challenge – finding a bike mechanic who could repair the completely flat tyres in under ten hours. They couldn't reveal why it was urgent, because the project was still a secret.

→ 12.08.24 / SAINT-MORITZ
The physiologists Jesús Álvarez-Herms and Sergi Cinca collected as many data points as possible before the start of the adventure. These would serve as the basis for several scientific studies.

THE TEAM

Although I completed this journey under my own power, I still received some assistance. Aina García, who has worked alongside me on numerous expeditions, from the Himalayas to the Pyrenees, was project leader. She ensured that I always had food and a place to sleep, and also managed the film crew. My mum, Núria, was also there. The first week she stayed with Emelie and the girls in Valais, and later joined Aina. David Ariño, Joel Badia and Nick Danielson filmed the journey. Towards the end, Noa Barrau, a friend of Mathéo Jacquemoud, joined the final stages to do some filming in the mountains as well. On the first two days, doctors Jesús Álvarez-Herms and Sergi Cinca recorded physiological and cognitive data when I descended between ranges to study the effects of these extreme events on my body. On certain days, other people came to help: Anouchka, Sofia, Joan and Andreu linked up with my twenty-strong team who were following remotely and handling press relations, logistics and more. I also called a few friends to see if they wanted to meet up to share sections of the journey with me.

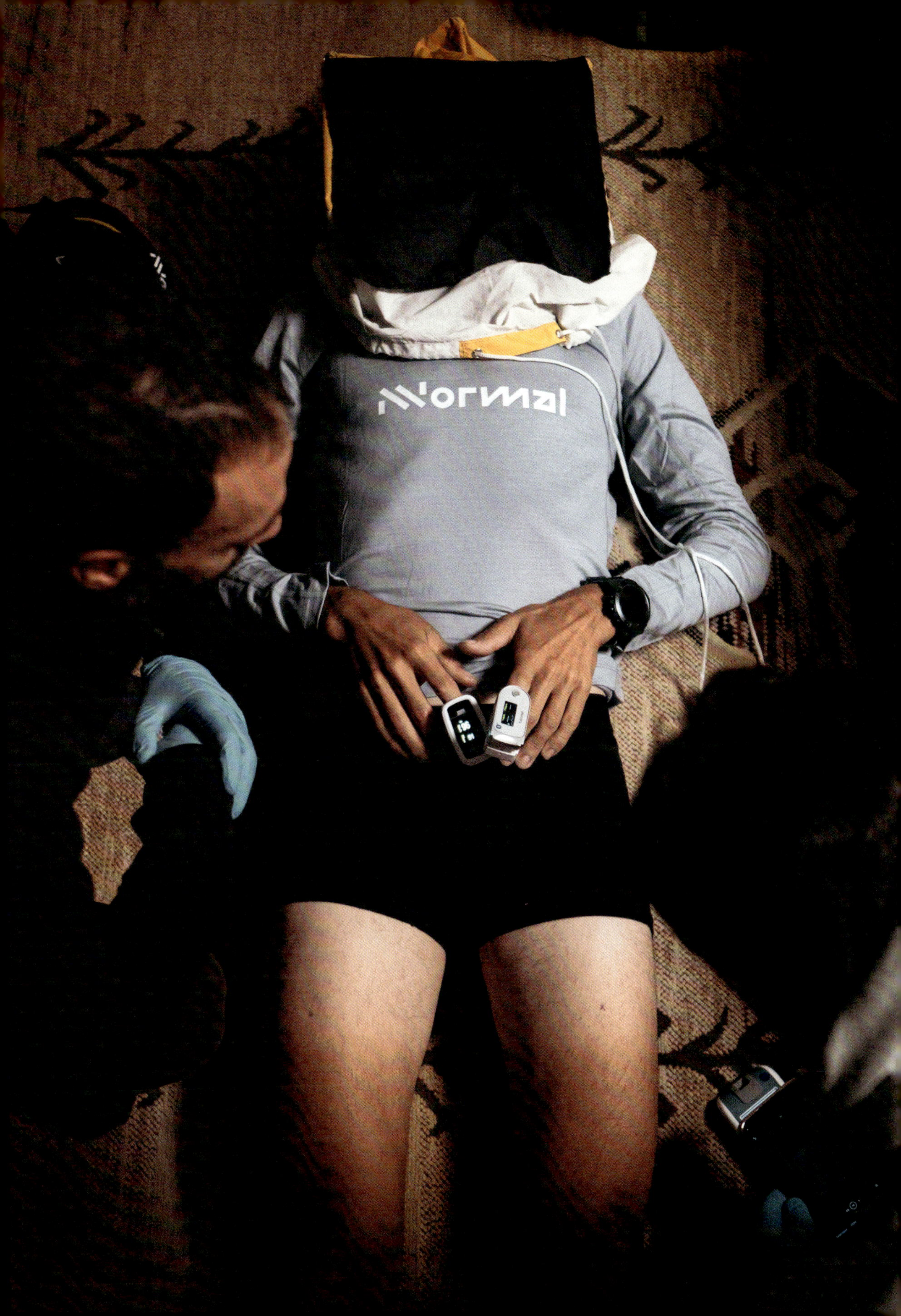
Normal

NNormal

← 12.08.24 / SAINT-MORITZ
All of my gear for this expedition.

grateful for the room and board offered, even if I got there quite late at night. The team members who accompanied and supported me along the way played an irreplaceable role. They brought all the supplies I needed when I was in the valleys and chronicled the journey with their camera – pictures that, to this day, make me emotional when I look at them, for their beauty, symbolism and motivational power.

I'm not proud of all the decisions that I took, not in the slightest. There are risks we expose ourselves to that aren't very reasonable, because they involve facing dangers with unpredictable consequences. I've done some inner work to try to understand the impulse that drives me to make overly risky choices that go beyond what is reasonable.

That said, all things considered, I got through it pretty well. From a physiological standpoint, I didn't lose any weight. In 2023, in the Pyrenees, it had been a completely different story: I suffered a constant physical decline at the time. Here in the Alps, I was able to keep on recovering and, in fact, I finished strong. I ate well and, relatively speaking, I got the rest I needed. These are two crucial points. It's also clear that I had prepared everything more thoroughly: I had planned, studied and revised the routes for several months. I had pored over every detail time and time again. I tried to leave as little as possible to improvisation, and although many elements were beyond my control, this preparation gave me a great deal of confidence during the journey.

THE GEAR

For footwear, I chose three pairs of Tomir 02 shoes – two waterproof pairs, which I wore most days, and a third pair that I used for one day while the others dried.

For clothing, from my feet to my head, I wore both waterproof and non-waterproof socks, one pair of thermal tights and a pair of Activ outerwear trousers. For my upper body, I brought a merino wool T-shirt, a midlayer, a windbreaker, a waterproof jacket, a down jacket, a Buff neck-gaiter and a beanie. I used climbing gloves (four pairs in total) made of synthetic leather to protect my hands against rock abrasion and I also had a pair of gaiters.

As always in the mountains, it's essential to protect ourselves from the sun, and I brought two pairs of category-four sunglasses, sunscreen and a SPF lip balm.

For mountaineering gear, I chose a helmet, a light harness, an ice screw, two ice axes, two trail running poles and a pair of crampons. On specific stages, I used a safety carabiner, rope and a carabiner, small cords and rope, an ice screw, an Abalakov thread and two stoppers. For night visibility, I had a headlamp and a spare battery.

For tracking and communication, I had a phone with all my maps, a Coros Vertix GPS watch, a tracking device, a GoPro, a portable charger as well as some cash for the mountain huts. For food and hydration, I carried two soft flasks and a few nutritious snacks.

All that had to fit in a 25–30 litre rucksack. On sections where I had to use the bike, the team handed me cycling kit, a helmet and a Coros Dura GPS bike computer.

I was able to climb with fluidity. On some ridges I didn't feel any tension at all, I just enjoyed the profound connection with the mountain. The effort faded away, time stood still, and my body became one with the environment. These are the great moments in life – it's for moments like these that I live.

To carry my project through and to keep moving forward, no matter the conditions, the weather or the gear I had, I had to make the best possible use of my knowledge, going beyond all the limits I had anticipated. The effort I put in was physical and technical of course, but above all, it was mental. Managing stress and emotions is always fundamental, but this time it was more important than ever.

What turned out to be the most challenging on this journey was staying fully concentrated for so many hours a day, and managing my stress in difficult situations to stay clear-headed, make good decisions and save my energy.

But what struck me the most was realizing that the Alps I once knew had changed considerably. I hadn't lived there for eight years, but the differences that I saw pained me. Like a runaway horse, climate change is galloping away unimpeded by anything in its path. The loss of glaciers and the thaw of the permafrost are considerable, irreversible changes. As a result, the access routes have changed and now the conditions to undertake them are much more dangerous. It hurts just thinking about it, but it's true: the mountains are falling apart, it's as simple as that.

The Alps are experiencing rapid transformations due to the rise in temperatures. Global warming is accelerating changes; it not only poses a threat to the beauty and biodiversity of the region, but it also creates enormous risks for athletes and anyone who loves the mountains.

We must urgently adopt sustainable practices and assist in conservation efforts to curb these harmful effects. If there is still time, protecting the Alps' unique ecosystems would give the chance for future generations to continue putting their limits to the test in these beautiful and inspiring landscapes.

Despite my deep concern for this climate and environmental disaster, I revelled in the beauty of nature. I witnessed breathtaking sunsets, full moons and crimson sunrises. There's still hope. I was fortunate enough to clasp magnificent stones – graceful dance partners that carried me onward with every step. I enjoyed long, wonderful hours of solitude, just as I shared laughs and ridges with friends. In the end, these are the moments that will stay with me for a long time.

↑ 12.08.24 / SAINT-MORITZ
As I knew the traverse would be highly demanding, I took care to verify all the gear, check the weight and make a rigorous selection to make it easier to use and transport.

→ 12.08.24 / SAINT-MORITZ
Physiological and cognitive data were collected at rest to check my condition before the start and then analyse their changes over time.

THE FIRST STEPS

STAGES:
1-3

1.	PIZ BERNINA	4049 m
2.	LAUTERAARHORN	4042 m
3.	SCHRECKHORN	4078 m
4.	FINSTERAARHORN	4274 m
5.	GROSS GRÜNHORN	4044 m
6.	HINTERES FIESCHERHORN	4025 m
7.	GROSSES FIESCHERHORN	4049 m
8.	MÖNCH	4107 m
9.	JUNGFRAU	4158 m
10.	ALETSCHHORN	4193 m

↑ **13.08.24/PIZ BERNINA**
The first summits at the beginning of the traverse, among them Piz Bernina (4,049 m/13,284 ft).

→ **13.08.24/PIZ BERNINA**
Descending the Piz Bernina at a good pace, thinking ahead about the next stage of the traverse to ensure an aesthetically pleasing connection.

↑ 13.08.24/PONTRESINA
Resting after the first section. Careful planning of nutrition was essential.

↗ The first section by bike was a long and demanding stage, having covered more than 200 kilometres (124 miles).

← 13.08.24/PIZ BERNINA
The adventure wasn't only about reaching the summit, but also maintaining control over my body and constant mental focus to continue traversing the other summits.

The sun still hadn't risen, and so we set in high spirits with our headlamps on. We climbed up the Piz Bernina, the easternmost four-thousander in the Alps, along the Spalla ridge, starting from Pontresina, taking a beautiful, uncomplicated route with varied terrain. We were greeted with great weather. It was perfect, the sun was pleasant and there was no wind. What more could I ask for! In these great conditions, Philipp and I enjoyed the climb and reaching the first summit all the more thanks to the views.

Once back at base, I picked up my bike and headed off on my own towards the Grimsel Pass, traversing iconic passes such as Oberalp and Furka, to reach the beginning of the next stage. It was a pleasant journey – tinged with the calm and serenity of the start.

I reached the Grimsel Pass with the fading light of day. The first setback was the result of human activity: I got stuck in an unexpected predicament, because some work was being done on the dam. Nevertheless, I found a good place to sleep and got a few hours rest. The scientific team caught up with me at

specific times to take physiological samples and cognitive assessments, such as my sleep patterns, in order to better understand what was happening during these efforts and how this could help people's performance and health.

The following day, a little before 5 a.m., I started the second stage by heading off to the Grimsel Pass to run the long – very long at 20 kilometres (12,425 miles) – Unteraargletscher moraine. The goal was to link the LAUTERAARHORN (4,042 m/13,261 ft) and the SCHRECKHORN (4,078 m/13,379 ft), two peaks joined by a ridge requiring serious climbing. It is no coincidence that *Shrecken* is the German word for 'terror'. This climb is considered one of the most technical and complicated in the world of mountaineering ever since the first ascent in 1861. After that, I continued towards the FINSTERAARHORN (4,274 m/14,022 ft), the highest peak in the Bernese Alps. It wasn't too difficult, but the terrain slowed me down even though I was only a little tired (I had managed to get four hours' sleep).

I started the ascent to the Lauteraarhorn at a good pace. It was a slow-moving climb; the ground was a combination of rocks, loose soil and soft snow. I was literally taking two steps forward and one step back. On the ridge, now on solid rock, I started to get worried about the storms: the forecasts called for lightning in the afternoon but, looking at the horizon, it seemed like it would arrive sooner.

I took the time for reflection. I wasn't sure whether to seek cover or to continue. I knew that once I started on the ascent of the ridge to the Schreckhorn, there would be precious few options for shelter. I decided to keep going. During the ascent, I was looking out for places where I could get rid of my metallic and electronic equipment and cavities to find shelter, should I need to.

The storm was coming from the west; it was a big one and the lightning was getting closer. I started to get stressed; I was having a tough time of it. Luckily, the storm passed a few hundred metres away and continued eastward.

After the storm...came the snow. So the last part of the ridge towards the Schreckhorn was quite damp and covered in snow, but the rock was excellent. Once I knew that no more lightning was coming my way and that the weather was giving me a break, the climb was fantastic and I ate heartily. The ridge is gorgeous with lovely views when the clouds cleared enough for me to see something. Once on the glacier, the sun rewarded me with an appearance and the afternoon ended up being a lot warmer than expected.

↑ 14.08.24/GRIMSEL
Despite the darkness and setting off or travelling at odd hours, what I remember most is the sensation of climbing those mountains – and feeling a connection with them.

← PP. 26–27
13.08.24/PONTRESINA
The bike route from Pontresina to the Grimsel Pass via the Furka Pass was lovely. It was the beginning of the adventure and the views were enchanting.

→ PP. 29–31
14.08.24/SCHRECKHORN
From our vantage points throughout the adventure, we witnessed firsthand the dangers the Alps face due to climate change, and how it is reshaping both the Alpine landscape and its structure.

→ PP. 32–33
14.08.24/SCHRECKHORN
Left: on the traverse I came across a lot of snow, which often slowed me down. I also encountered unexpected weather conditions, like the lightning storm which forced me to seek shelter in a mountain hut.
Right: during the climbing hours, often without a break – up to seventeen hours non-stop – keeping safe and work with the rock was paramount.

The crossing of the Schreckhorn Glacier to the Finsteraarhorn was far from easy: long stretches of moraine, sections of climbing, and near the summit a route winding through crevasses. From there, I set out on a long couloir until Agassizjoch. Due to the thaw, crossing the Bergschrund (large crevasse) was tough, but I managed to enter the couloir and ascend on the right face of the rock. One half was covered with soft snow, the other with rock. From there, at the start of the ridge that led to the Finsteraarhorn, the rock was quite loose all the way to the junction with the normal route. I got there late afternoon. Right after that another snowstorm hit, which caused the last stretch to the top to be particularly slippery.

It was already late night when I finally reached the hut on the Finsteraarhorn. Luckily, the hut wardens were waiting for me there. After such a hard day, seeing friendly faces is so comforting. On top of this, if you're greeted with a hot vegetable soup, then it's not just the high altitude that gives you the feeling that you're touching the sky. After that warm and comforting welcome, I tried to go to sleep.

After two hours of rest on this second day of the second stage, I put on my wet shoes and crossed the glacier in the direction of Grünhornlücke, towards the east and through the normal route until reaching GROSS GRÜNHORN (4,044 m/13,268 ft). The magnificent sunrise was a sight to behold. The rain and snow from the previous night made the rock slippery. Instead of continuing along the ridge, I descended halfway along the glacier on the west side and I trekked towards the Grünhornlücke.

The rock at the start of the ridge was quite poor, though further up it became more solid and offered a pleasant, straight and long climb up to HINTERES FIESCHERHORN (4,025 m/13,205 ft). I quickly crossed towards GROSSES FIESCHERHORN (4,049 m/13,284 ft) before I descended the north ridge and the long high plateau of the glacier until reaching the mountain hut at Mönch. I ate, then I climbed and descended the well-trodden MÖNCH (4,107 m/13,474 ft). It has a beautiful rocky climb and a narrow snowy ridge with marvellous views of the Bernese Alps.

After so much time alone, it was a shock to suddenly come across thousands of people at the Jungfraujoch, which has been turned into a tourist centre that's easily accessed by train. Through overcrowded tunnels, I found the exit for the JUNGFRAU GLACIER (4,158 m/13,642 ft). It was late afternoon and we could see the green valleys to the north from the summit. According to local lore, the Eiger, Mönch and Jungfrau mountains symbolize an ogre, a monk and a young girl. The Eiger wanted to capture the

↑↑ 15.08.24/MÖNCH MOUNTAIN HUT
The team joined me at the Mönch shelter, where we sorted the gear for the next stages and had some food.

↑ I had planned to arrive in the middle of the night, but I got there at lunchtime, when the dining room was full of people. While Nick did a quick interview, there were tourists watching everything.

→ 15.08.24/MÖNCH MOUNTAIN HUT
Descending from the Mönch hut to Saas-Grund.

←↑ 15.08.24 / MÖNCH MOUNTAIN HUT
These hours of activity were crucial.
I started testing my physical and technical limits, as well as my overall systemic stress.

Jungfrau, but the Mönch stood in his way to protect her, and that's why Mönch is in the middle, keeping the other two apart. This story has inspired tales, paintings and local products. Memories from my two previous expeditions here came to mind: in 2007, during the European Championships of Ski Mountaineering in Grindelwald, and in 2015, when I scaled the north face of the Eiger with Ueli Steck, who was doing his own traverse across the Alps, which then became one of my sources of inspiration.

I went down to Jungfraufirn, crossing large crevasses and snow bridges which, despite their apparent fragility, allowed me to move forward with assurance until Konkordiaplatz, a major confluence point where the ice from various glaciers comes together to form a vast plain of snow and ice. From there, I went in the direction of the north face of the ALETSCHHORN (4,193 m/13,756 ft). I had aimed to scale the north spur and the northeast ridge, but while I was heading to the base a hard rain started falling and I had to turn tail. Everything was damp and I was soaked from head to toe. It was freezing and night was just about to fall.

↑↗ 15.08.24/JUNGFRAU
The summit of Jungfrau has become quite touristy thanks to the cable car. The contrast between this crowded summit and the immensity of the mountains is remarkable. This ascent was part of the third stage of the project, which included six peaks and an elevation gain of 8,778 metres (28,799 feet).

So I headed down to the south face, hoping for the rain to stop and find a drier route. The exit from the Aletsch Glacier was incredibly long. The path to traverse it wasn't as straight as I had imagined, because there were two enormous crevasses. At least the rising moon illuminated a fantastic view. First, I thought I would stay on the right side of the glacier to go up along the northeast ridge but, at night, I didn't know how to find an easy route to leave the glacier and I thought it was best not to lose time and energy trying to get there. I decided to go down to the end of the glacier and come back onto the normal ascent route. Thankfully, the rain subsided and, even though it was night, my clothes dried a bit from the movement and I wasn't too cold.

In moments like this – when you have the goal within reach, but you know that you won't be able to get there and you have to change course, making the route much longer and adding extra hours – it's essential to manage your frustration and energy expenditure. It's disappointing of course, but deep down I know that this is also part of the mountain challenge, and you have to

→ PP. 40–45
15.08.24 / JUNGFRAU
During the *Alpine Connections* project, I was once again reminded of what the mountain teaches us: patience and the ability to wait for the opportune moment. You can plan ahead all you want – in the end the mountains decide.

‘When Kilian returns to base, he can return to being a husband, a father, and a teammate. It’s very inspiring.’

EMELIE FORSBERG

Emelie Forsberg is an athlete, a ski mountaineer, one of the pioneers of women’s trail running and an advocate for mindful living. She is a two-time world champion and holds numerous mountaineering records. She is an inspiration to many women around the world on how to connect with nature and push their limits. Emilie is also Kilian’s wife and the mother of their three daughters (their third daughter was born in 2025).

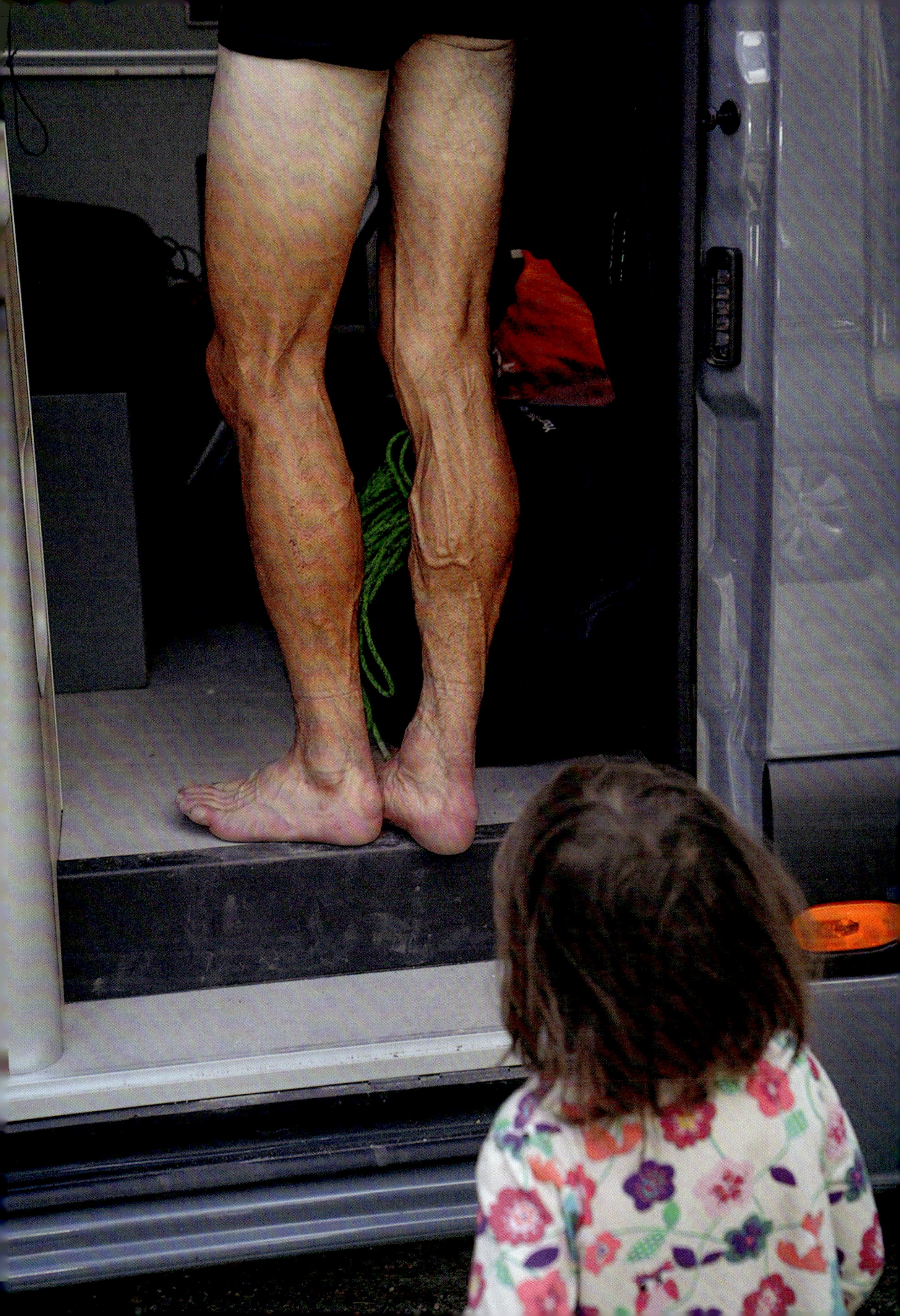

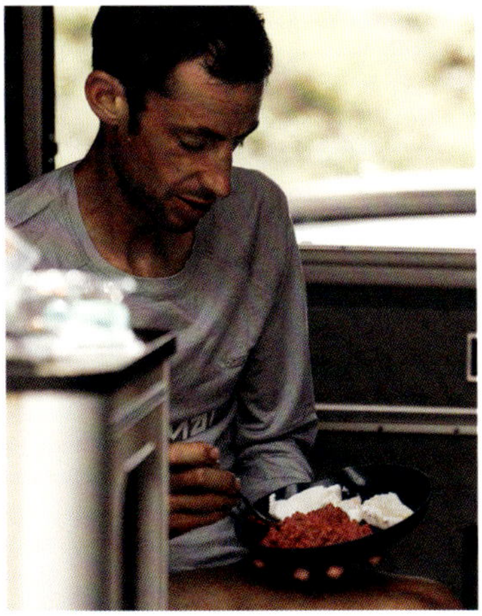

↑ 16.08.24/BLATTEN BEI NATERS
After climbing the first summits of the Oberland stage, I needed to recover my strength to take on the second section by bike, which I completed with Jordi. We rode 40 kilometres (25 miles) downhill until Saas-Fee, to link up to the start of the next stage.

← 16.08.24/BLATTEN BEI NATERS
On the descent journey from the Aletschhorn, the whole team came to meet me in the small village of Blatten bei Naters.

such as the Pierra Menta and the Rutor, and he also joined me on some incredible journeys through the Alps, including one across the Aravis Range, and we also did the rapid ascent to Mont Blanc together. Since then, we've always stayed in contact and that's why I was so pleased to see him in the mountains after all this time. It gave us the opportunity to catch up on our family news as well Mathéo's work at the National Skiing and Mountaineering School and with elite athletes.

When we reached the hut, looking at the weather, we decided it was better to climb the WEISSMIES (4,017 m/13,179 ft), marking the beginning of the fourth stage (see page 55). The sun kept us company as we started to cross the glacier and continued up to the summit as quickly as we could among the hordes of people climbing there too.

Upon reaching the summit, Mathéo started getting his paraglider ready, which he would use to descend. As he was doing that, I snacked on a sandwich while watching him check every last detail. Once ready, making the most of perfect weather conditions, he leaped into the air while I set off running down the glacier, a much longer and less entertaining adventure than his aerial one. We had planned to meet back at the bottom.

Next, we climbed up Lagginjoch and the southern ridge of the LAGGINHORN (4,010 m/13,156 ft), a more interesting trail than the normal one. It's also one of the easiest: the ground is dry and there's a trail so the descent was easy enough. It offers enchanting views of the Valais mountains on one side and the Italian high plateau on the other. Once back at Saas-Grund, I had dinner with Emelie and the girls, and we said goodbye for now. While they headed back up north, I took my bicycle and rode all the way to Saas-Fee, to continue trekking the Alps to the east. Having trekked for only eight hours, with the added bonus of a family meal, it almost seemed like a rest day to me. It helped me to recover my strength after the strenuous efforts of the previous days.

During the first three stages, I had accumulated nearly 20,000 metres (65,100 feet) of elevation gain, summited 10 peaks, achieved 67.5 hours of sustained effort and travelled some 425 kilometres (264 miles). Despite the unexpected setbacks, I felt strong and full of anticipation for the days that were still to come.

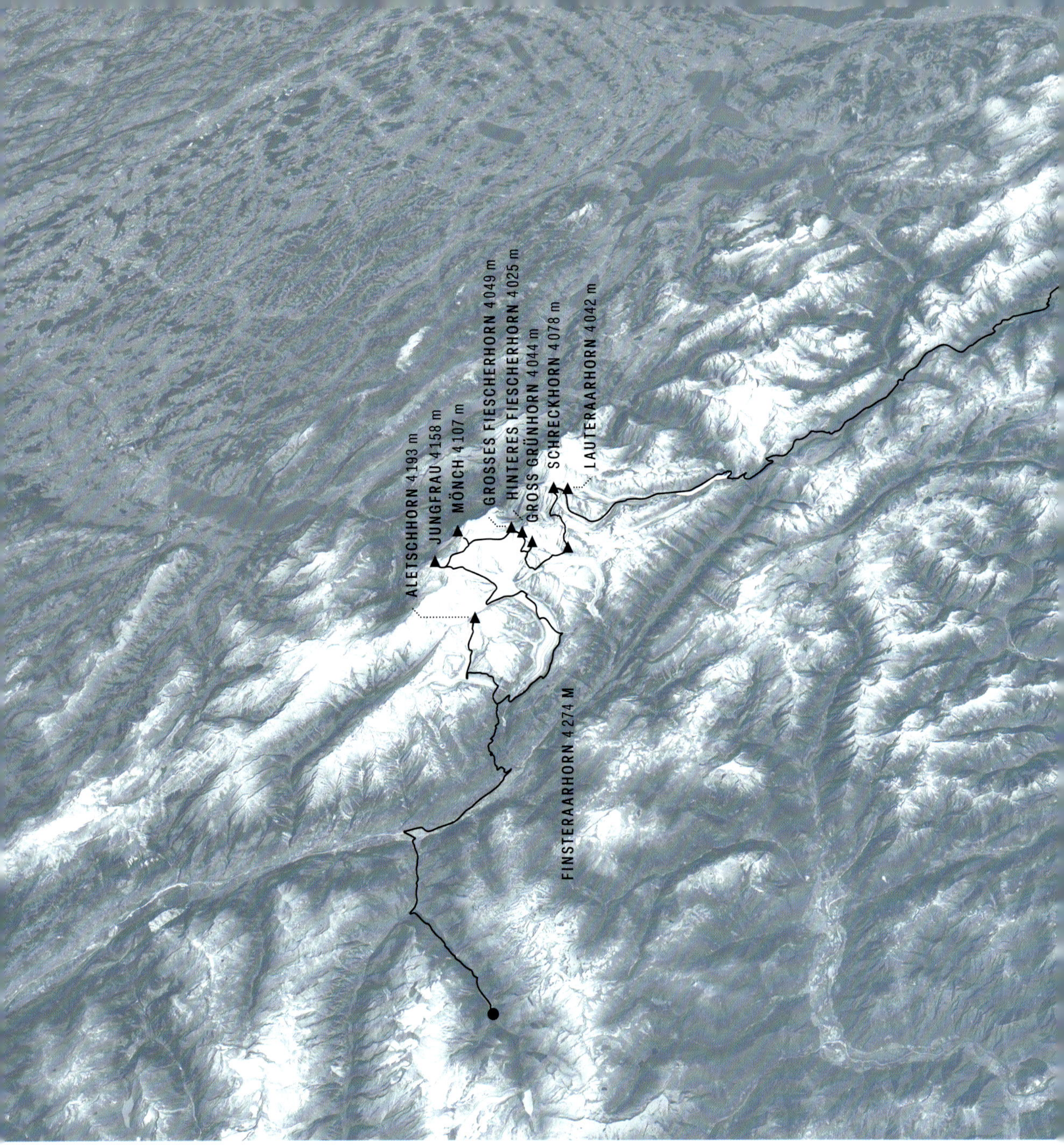

STAGES:
1–3

CLIMBING
BIKING

TOTAL PEAKS > 4,000 m (13,123 ft):
10

TOTAL ELEVATION GAIN:
19,831 m/65,062 ft

TOTAL DISTANCE:
424.73 km/264 miles

TOTAL SLEEP:
10:45:00

TOTAL ACTIVITY:
67:27:09

PIZ BERNINA 4 049 m

ELEVATION:

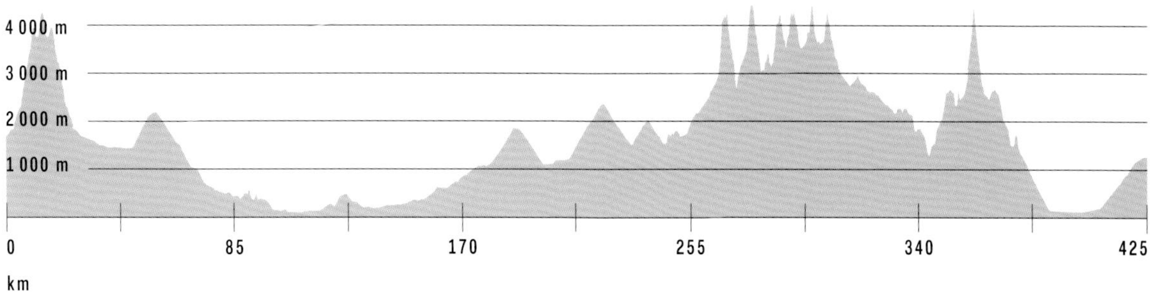
4 000 m
3 000 m
2 000 m
1 000 m
0
85
170
255
340
425
km

RESILIENCE

STAGES:
4–9

11.	LAGGINHORN	4 010 m
12.	WEISSMIES	4 017 m
13.	DÜRRENHORN	4 035 m
14.	HOHBERGHORN	4 219 m
15.	STECKNADELHORN	4 241 m
16.	NADELHORN	4 327 m
17.	LENZSPITZE	4 294 m
18.	DOM	4 545 m
19.	TÄSCHHORN	4 491 m
20.	ALPHUBEL	4 206 m
21.	ALLALINHORN	4 027 m
22.	RIMPFISCHHORN	4 199 m
23.	STRAHLHORN	4 190 m
24.	NORDEND	4 609 m
25.	DUFOURSPITZE	4 634 m
26.	ZUMSTEINSPITZE	4 563 m
27.	SIGNALKUPPE	4 554 m
28.	PARROTSPITZE	4 432 m
29.	LUDWIGSHÖHE	4 341 m
30.	SCHWARZHORN	4 322 m
31.	VINCENT PYRAMID	4 215 m
32.	PUNTA GIORDANI	4 046 m
33.	EASTERN LYSKAMM	4 527 m
34.	WESTERN LYSKAMM	4 479 m
35.	CASTOR	4 223 m
36.	POLLUX	4 092 m
37.	ROCCIA NERA	4 075 m
38.	BREITHORN	4 106 m
39.	EASTERN BREITHORN	4 139 m
40.	CENTRAL BREITHORN	4 159 m
41.	WESTERN BREITHORN	4 164 m
42.	MATTERHORN	4 478 m
43.	DENT D'HÉRENS	4 171 m
44.	DENT BLANCHE	4 357 m
45.	OBER GABELHORN	4 063 m
46.	ZINALROTHORN	4 221 m
47.	WEISSHORN	4 505 m
48.	BISHORN	4 153 m

55

As I explore my limits in the Alps, these mountains that I love so dearly, I realize that these ecosystems are coming closer to their own limits. Nature is becoming smaller because of us, and it is estimated that, since the first time I came to the Alps about twenty years ago, the mountains' glaciers have lost nearly 40 per cent of their volume. Climate change has had devastating effects on these mountains. The loss of glacial mass not only impacts the Alpine landscape and ecosystem, but it also affects the availability of fresh water and the generation of hydroelectric power, and contributes to rising water levels.

These concerns weighed on my mind as I consulted the weather forecasts to take on the Valais stage. The conditions were so unfavourable that I considered taking a break from the *Alpine Connections* for a day. In the end, I decided to go up and check if the fallen snow would be an obstacle for me to continue.

The first destination was the historic Mischabel mountain hut, a typical starting point for ascents to the NADELHORN (4,327 m/14,196 ft). In an ancient German dialect, *Mischabel* means 'pitchfork'. The highest peaks are bunched closely together, forming as it were a structure similar to a pitchfork. This mountain hut, which nowadays comprises two buildings at an altitude of 3,340 metres (10,958 feet), dates back to 1902.

I had slept well, so I set off at daybreak. The ascent was direct so it didn't take me too long to reach the glacier. I crossed it and managed to reach the Nadelhorn along the ridge. There had been heavy snow, with a cumulative depth of around 15 centimetres (6 inches). While taking in the views, I felt a sense of nostalgia for my adopted Norwegian landscapes and yet I felt somehow completely at home, with the wind, the snow, and the rocky ridges, and that small patch of blue in the sky which meant I could call this a sunny day.

I descended through the Nadelgrat ridge until the DÜRRENHORN (4,035 m/13,238 ft), but recent rockslides created hazardous conditions. So I decided it was best to turn around. When I got back to the Mischabel mountain hut, I was pleasantly surprised to run into Ed Albrighi, a mountain guide and skyrunner who left behind London's financial scene to live in the Alps. Ed greeted me with a hot chocolate, and as soon as we regained our strength, we ran together towards Saas-Fee.

There, Mathéo joined me once again on the adventure and all together we ascended the northeast ridge to reach the LENZSPITZE (4,294 m/14,088 ft). The snow was fresh and the rocks

↑ 17.08.24/SAAS-FEE
The key was to get some rest and a few hours of sleep, as the stages started very early, sometimes at 3.30 a.m., with my headlamp on and full of excitement.

→ 17.08.24/WEISSMIES GLACIER
One of the great rewards of this adventure was being able to share climbing experiences with friends, like climbing the Weissmies Glacier with Mathéo, who shared many moments of the traverse with me.

← P. 54
19.08.24/LENZSPITZE SOUTH ARÊTE
After four intense days, I decided to plot a new route on the map: the stage through the Weissmies massif, near Saas-Fee, in Switzerland.

↑ 17.08.24/WEISSMIES GLACIER
Step by step, we advance towards the summits of the fourth stage.

↗ It was always important to take a break to adjust layers and review the route.

← 17.08.24/WEISSMIES GLACIER
The Weissmies Glacier, with its clearly marked trail, reveals the mark of our presence in the high mountains, a visual reminder of how our behaviour impacts the planet.

→ PP. 60–61
17.08.24/LAGGINHORN
I was struck by the contrast between the soft snow, the majestic glaciers, the ice walls, and the bare rock of the drier zones.

↑ 17.08.24/LAGGINHORN
My *Petite balade alpine* gave me the opportunity to chart a unique route, such as climbing the Lagginhorn via the south face.

↑ 17.08.24/LAGGINHORN
After the ascent of the Lagginhorn, Mathéo decided to call it a day and took off with his paraglider, while I ran down to the valley.

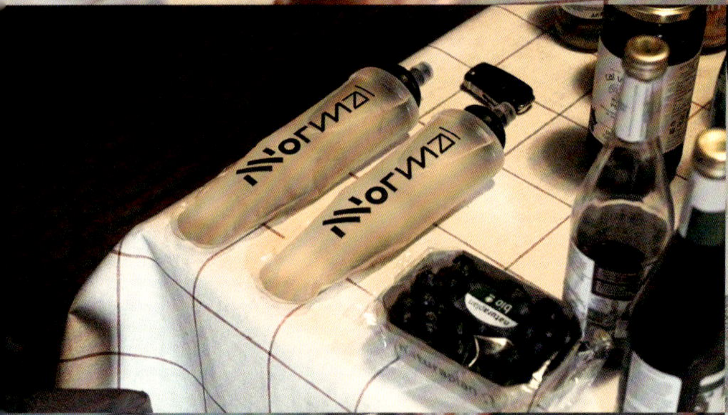

↑ 17.08.24/SAAS-GRUND

A seemingly short but intense stage: 7 hours and 29 minutes to do 30 kilometres (18.6 miles), with 3,381 metres (11,092 feet) of elevation gain. Earlier, a good start: preparing the gear, checking the weather forecast, eating properly... then start a new day of effort and discovery.

→ PP. 68–69

19.08.24/MISCHABEL MOUNTAIN HUT

After losing my mobile phone on a stage in the Pyrenees, I now have a case with a lanyard and a carabiner to prevent this from happening again. In the dark, I often encountered mountain goats.

↑ 19.08.24/MISCHABEL MOUNTAIN HUT
On the descent, I once again stopped at the mountain hut to eat something before returning to Saas-Fee.

← 19.08.24/MISCHABEL MOUNTAIN HUT
Ensuring a coherent connection – both physically and visually – between the ridges and the summits was fundamental to my route.

↑ 19.08.24/MISCHABEL MOUNTAIN HUT
The first stage in the Valais had a key location: the Mischabel mountain hut, which allowed me to complete four more peaks.

slippery, which made climbing quite tricky. We thought we were doing quite well on the orange granite, but the surroundings were hostile: a thick fog covered us as we climbed the DOM (4,545 m/14,911 ft), the highest peak in the Mischabel. 'Dom' comes from the German word for cathedral – hence perhaps its imposing presence.

In those conditions, we had to open a deep track in the glacier. The weather was showing no signs of improvement. From the Dom, the ridge that leads to the TÄSCHHORN (4,491 m/14,734 ft) is long and covered in snow almost the entire route, so we had to rope ourselves together. The terrain was easy, but we were quite exposed. We took a quick break to pay homage to the legendary French mountaineer Patrick Berhault, who died right there, on one of these cornices in 2004. The wind then dissipated our sadness and the fog lifted enough to allow us to see towers of black rock emerging among the fading clouds; it was like watching an animated film.

We descended by a ridge until we reached Mischabeljoch and we climbed the ALPHUBEL (4,206 m/13,799 ft), where we encountered

↑ 19.08.24/MISCHABEL MASSIF
The start of the second stage in the Valais started under a sky heavy with rain and snow. The typical 'Norwegian' weather makes me feel right at home.

↗ Mathéo and I had planned to link the stunning peaks of the Mischabel massif: Lenzspitze, Dom and Täschhorn.

a ray of sunlight, as well as Genís Zapater, a mountain enthusiast, and his friend Bryce. The five of us continued until the ALLALINHORN (4,027 m/13,212 ft), where Mathéo and Bryce decided to go back down. Mathéo, ever loyal to his passion, took this chance to jump off with his inseparable paraglider.

With Genís we continued towards the Allalinpass, along a fairly unstable rocky ridge. We left some gear there and ran towards the RIMPFISCHHORN (4,199 m/13,776 ft). Night came upon us, and I ended up doing the climb solo guided by the full moon rising high above the Italian plateau.

During the descent from the Alderpass towards the Adler, Findel and Gorner Glaciers, heading for the Monte Rossa mountain hut, I got quite a scare. Going down a flat glacier, I tripped with my crampons and fell face first on the hard, flat black ice. The gear I had in my chest pocket, a GoPro and a GPS tracker, crushed me violently and one of my ribs started hurting. At the time, I didn't know if I had broken it or just cracked it (which turned out to be the case). But what I was certain of – because it was not the first time this had happened to me – was that for the

→ PP. 76–79
19.08.24/MISCHABEL MASSIF
Keeping to our goals also meant accepting what was beyond our control: the condition of the rock and the weather.

← 19.08.24/ALLALINHORN
Alpine Connections has been the adventure of a lifetime, and what a joy to share it with friends and family.

towards Monte Rosa, the most extensive massif in the Alps. It's home to the DUFOURSPITZE (4,634 m/15,203 ft), the second highest peak in the Alps after Mont Blanc.

Sometimes we make mistakes, and that was certainly the case for me that day. I thought I'd find many established tracks that would allow me to run with ease through the glaciers, but that wasn't the case. So, from NORDEND (4,609 m/15,121 ft), I had to make my own route. The same thing happened to me between the Dufourspitze and the ZUMSTEINSPITZE (4,563 m/14,970 ft). I made a pit stop at the Margherita hut, on the summit of the SIGNALKUPPE (4,554 m/14,941 ft), to eat and drink.

After two days without hardly seeing anyone bar my team, I realized that as I was getting on with this stage, there were quite a lot of people at the peaks now that I was starting to go up. Since they're easy to access and don't require much technical expertise, they've become quite popular. The path that I followed is known as the 'spaghetti tour', due to its shape and the fact that it is located in the Italian part, where the numerous huts serve up delicious pasta. It starts from the Monte Rosa mountain hut and links eighteen four-thousanders until BREITHORN (4,106 m/13,471 ft). Most are fairly easy to reach; you just go up and over the glacier. But that day it was really hot, and the snow was melting quickly. Because the snow and ice were melting, holes were opening up under my feet, slowing and complicating my progress.

As I was crossing EASTERN LYSKAMM (4,527 m/14,852 ft), a narrow, stunning snow-lined crest, I received an unexpected call: it was the Norwegian police. I answered worriedly, thinking that something had happened to Emelie or the girls. Thankfully, it wasn't anything serious, just a routine matter. I breathed a sigh of relief! They told me that, before setting off on my adventure, I had parked my car in a parking area where works were about to start and it needed to be moved. Obviously, that was impossible! I was very far away and I was otherwise busy... What could I do? Running between one ridge and the next in order to find a signal, I managed to call the car park manager to ask him to move my car. But he didn't have the keys, and just when we thought all hope was lost, he recalled that my car could be unlocked and started via an app. Seen from the outside, the situation was comical: I was high up on a ridge trying to find a signal to start my car parked in Norway so the police could move it elsewhere. In the end, we did it! It was a complete success, and it remains a fun memory.

Now that I had regained my composure, I proceeded to WESTERN LYSKAMM (4,479 m/14,695 ft) and crossed CASTOR (4,223 m/13,855 ft).

↑ 20.08.24/EASTERN LYSKAMM
The police want me to move my car... Here I am, 2,500 km (1,550 miles) from home, at an elevation of 4,000 metres (13,123 feet), in the middle of an 18-summit traverse.

↑ **21.08.24/VALAIS VALLEY**
At 7 a.m. I started one of the most demanding days of the project: the legendary 'spaghetti tour'.

→ **21.08.24/VALAIS VALLEY**
The snow was soft and with each step I sank almost 20 cm (8 inches), an additional challenge on this stretch of the adventure.

From POLLUX (4,092 m/13,425 ft), I headed off towards the traverse of the BREITHORN'S EASTERN SUMMIT (4,139 m/13,579 ft). I was exhausted, not to mention hungry and thirsty. Passing by the Rossi e Volante bivouac, I was lucky to run into a couple of mountaineers who were making dinner. When they saw the state I was in, they offered to share four boiled carrots and a little of their water with me. That incredibly simple meal was a godsend.

The last light of the day left an orange hue on the landscape. Awaiting me, I had a pleasant climb on solid rock that wasn't too difficult. The descent proved more arduous, and I was trying my best to avoid having to rappel. When night had fallen completely, I arrived at the summit of WESTERN BREITHORN (4,164 m/13,661 ft) – a place I hold dear to my heart, the first four-thousander that I climbed when I was only six years old with my parents and sister.

I ran down the ski slopes of Zermatt all the way to the Theodul Glacier Lake and, from there, I made my way to the Hörnli mountain hut. In my tired state, the trail had seemed long and I had felt worn down all through the day. Thankfully, my mother and Aina were waiting for me at the mountain hut, and they were still awake when I arrived. We shared a nice time and a good meal together. I then slept soundly for a couple of hours – enough to regain my strength.

I awoke on the ninth day of this adventure excited about a new stage, and I headed off towards the MATTERHORN (4,478 m/14,692 ft) after breakfast. I started slowly, but, as I was feeling pretty good, I increased the pace and ascended swiftly. The conditions were spectacular, with minimal snow, and there were wide tracks in the snow. It was windy though, that's for sure. Even though I thought the mountain would be busy, I only ran into a dozen teams.

After eating at the Carrel mountain hut – a wholehearted thank you to the Cervinia guides! – I skirted around the Testa del Leone before starting the long ridge leading to the DENT D'HÉRENS (4,171 m/13,684 ft). I have a lot of fond memories here, because I had climbed it with François Cazzanelli seven years prior to link the Grandes and Petites Murailles. I felt those same sensations coming back to me.

I was surprised to discover some footprints in places as it's not a very frequently traversed route. When I met up with Rolf Zurbrügg and one of his clients at the Aosta mountain shelter, I understood where the tracks had come from. I was happy to see him there. We first met back when Rolf was the trainer of the Swiss ski mountaineering team. We had a joyful meal together,

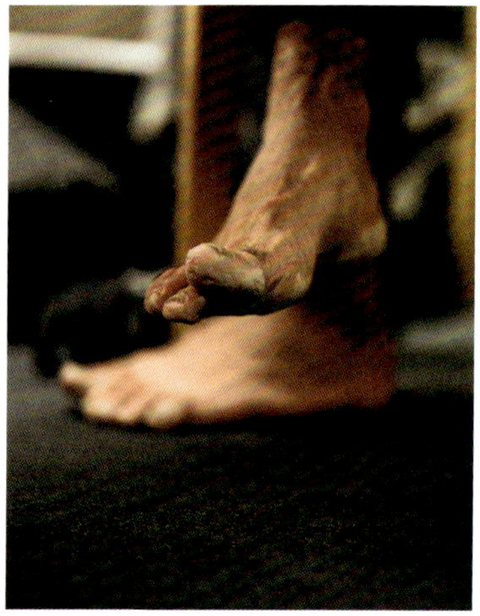

↑ 21.08.24 / HÖRNLI MOUNTAIN HUT
Thanks to the supermoon, I completed the stage in 17 hours and 45 minutes and I arrived at the hut at 1 a.m. Aina and Núria were waiting for me there and had prepared a surprise banquet. After dinner I went to sleep, exhausted.

→ 21.08.24 / ZERMATT
Starting my ascent of the mythical Matterhorn, the summit I ascended in 2013 via the iconic Lion arête route in a record time of 2 hours and 52 minutes.

↑ 22.08.24 / SCHÖNBIELHÜTTE
In addition to enjoying the mountains, one of the best moments was when I took a break to rest and share a meal with the team. Here I am with Mathéo, Joan, Andreu and Noa.

← 21.08.24 / MATTERHORN
After eating breakfast, feeling rested, I began the ascent. I moved quickly and nimbly, in good shape and full of energy.

← PP. 92–93
21.08.24 / MATTERHORN
The wonder of early departures: spectacular sunrises.

catching up on each other's news. Right after that, I headed off towards the Colle della Divisione before it was too late.

Genís and Bryce accompanied me to the Tête Blanche Glacier. The last time I had done this crossing was in 2015; I had spent several hours there and suffered quite a lot. This time went a lot more smoothly as the snow was compact and the progress was quick. The cherry on top was the stunning sunset we saw as we reached the Cabane de la Dent Blanche.

It was dinner time, and the hut warden, George, whipped up a magnificent mushroom risotto. After dinner, with Genís and Mathéo, who had joined us with his friend Noa, we continued up to the peak of DENT BLANCHE (4,357 m/14,295 ft). That ridge is wonderful, with solid, perfect rocks. I had already climbed this route a few times, on my own or with Emelie. This time, though, I was taken aback by the lack of snow on the ridge. Another reminder of the ravages of climate change. The full moon lit up the route and outlined the incredible skyline of the Valais mountains.

We descended along the same trail. Noa decided to return to the mountain hut, while Mathéo, Genis and I continued our descent via a steep spur towards the Schönbiel Glacier. We arrived at the Schönbielhütte mountain hut at the first light of dawn. Our team members Joan and Andreu were waiting for us there with sandwiches they had prepared for us.

After an hour's sleep, Mathéo and I continued running through the valley until we reached Arbenbiwak. The views were phenomenal, with the sun shining on the north face of the Matterhorn behind us. We spotted a few people ahead of us on the Arbengrat ridge, one of the Alps classics, with its perfect rock. We ate at the top and admired the views before starting our descent along the north ridge to the Wellenkuppe. It's a very comprehensive route; the climbing alternates rock and snow.

At Rothornhütte, Mathéo left me and I continued in the direction of the ZINALROTHORN (4,221 m/13,848 ft). There I met up with Björn Kruse, the mountain guide from Romsdal in Norway, with whom I had skied, climbed and written a book on skiing in our respective mountains.

It was starting to get late, and when I arrived at L'Épaule, there were only five hours left until sunset. My aim was to complete the ascent of the southern ridge of the WEISSHORN (4,505 m/14,780 ft) before nightfall. Before then, I had to cross the two peaks on the Moming, which aren't too demanding, and a steep icy path towards the Schalihorn, which leads to a long ridge until the Schalijoch and its small mountain hut, where you can sleep.

↑ 22.08.24/IMPERIAL CROWN

Although I had anticipated its physical and technical challenges, the mountain surprised me by demanding even more of me.

→ PP. 98–99

22.08.24/WEISSHORN

I felt as light as a cloud as I climbed along the ridge.

↑ 22.08.24/SCHÖNBIEL MOUNTAIN HUT
The crossing of the Valais was so technically demanding that eating and staying properly hydrated were crucial. I was beginning to feel the buildup of fatigue.

← 22.08.24/WEISSHORN
The setting sun to the west and the rising clouds to the east formed a Brocken spectre that followed me, faithfully reflecting my movements.

Despite the exertion, I was feeling good, most probably due to the build-up of adrenaline. When I arrived at the bivouac, I breathed a sigh of relief, because I still had two hours to scale the southern ridge before it got dark. I didn't have time to chat with the German team who were cooking and getting ready for the next day's climb. I left very quickly.

The Weisshorn remains one of my favourite mountains in the Alps. The trail to the summit isn't easy and, that's why, when it was conquered in 1861, it didn't have the immediate consequence of popularizing the climb, unlike with the other Alpine mountains at the same period. This majestic mountain has a perfect pyramid shape, with long ridges on each side.

What I experienced up there during my *Alpine Connections* expedition will stay with me my entire life. I felt like I was floating, as if a cloud was gently carrying me up to the crest of the ridge. The sunset in the west and the clouds in the east conjured up a Brocken spectre that followed me throughout the climb, mirroring all my movements in the sky as if in a reflection. My shadow, projected on the fog by the low sunlight, was surrounded by a circle of soft colours, a kind of ethereal halo that danced with me at every step – a ghostly reflection created by the magic of light and suspended water droplets. There were moments when I didn't know if I was awake or in a dream.

Reaching the summit, I was greeted by one of the most beautiful sunsets I've ever seen. And I've seen quite a few incredible ones! I caught my breath and started to downclimb the north ridge, which is no small feat – it involves scaling on rocky outcrops through gendarmes, and thin, jutting rock formations.

I was tired, so I decided to descend by the steeper slope to save time. That turned out to be a terrible decision. Either the darkness prevented me from finding the best path, or the ledges were set on rock that crumbled easily. Whatever the case, I had to be super focused so I wouldn't fall and take the mountain down with me. It took me a few hours to settle and proceed to the ascent to the BISHORN (4,153 m/13,625 ft).

I finally managed to get all the way down to the Tracuit mountain hut. The wardens had prepared a nice hot meal. I wolfed it down and then ran towards Zinal with Nick, who had come all this way to do some filming. It had only been a week since I had been in Zinal for the race. I was back there, slower and more tired than a week prior. But I was happy because I had completed the Imperial Crown of Valais, and with it the ascent of forty-eight peaks. We were just over halfway to our goal: the eighty-two four-thousanders in the Alps.

‘This expedition is unlike any of the previous projects. Kilian’s demands have been so extreme that it’s impossible for us to predict the physiological – and even genetic – changes that might occur.’

DOCTOR JESÚS ÁLVAREZ-HERMS

Jesús Álvarez-Herms holds a PhD in biomedicine and is an expert in physiology. He monitored Kilian and collected data during the entire traverse. He has worked with Kilian on various previous projects.

01:08

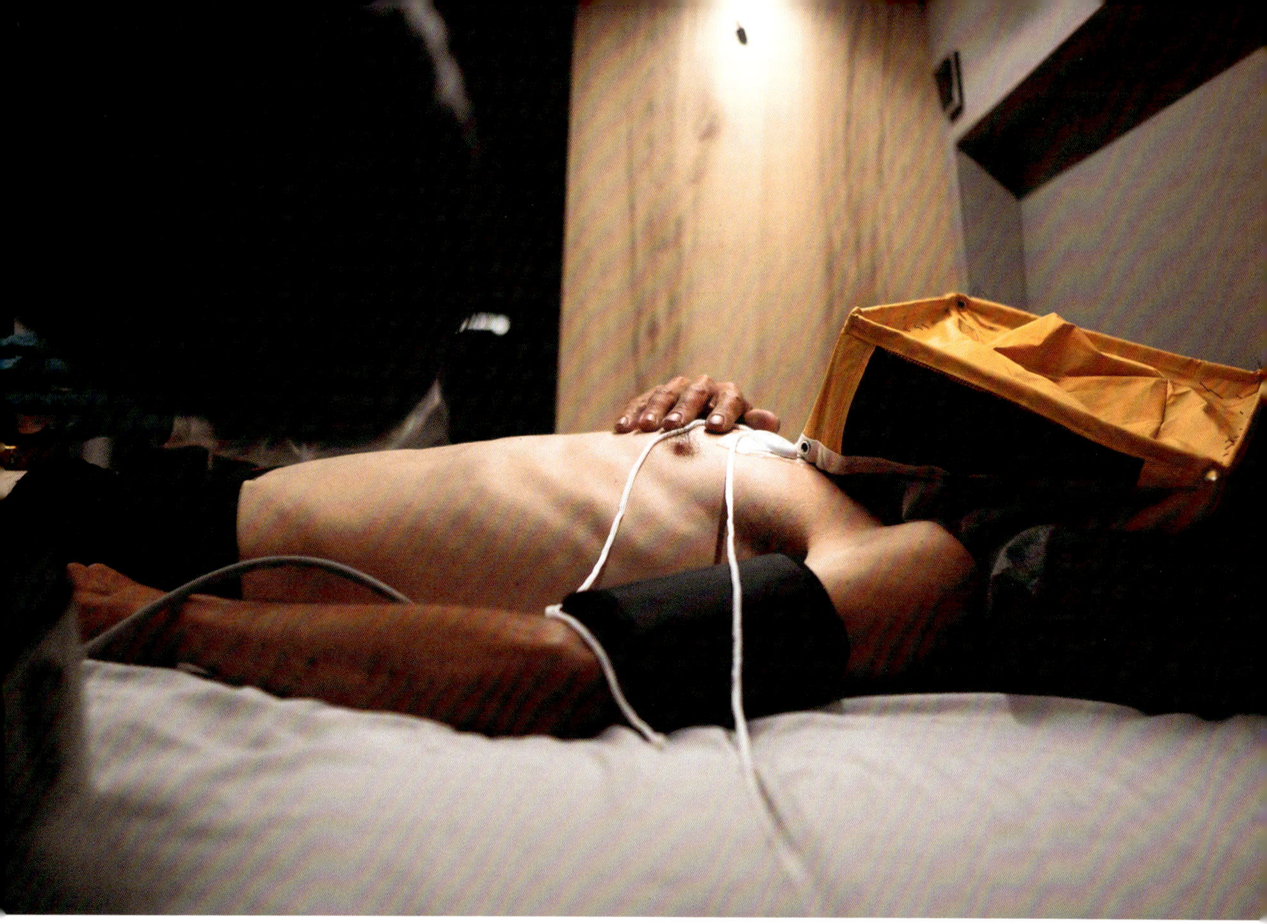

↑→ 22.08.24/ZINAL
The day and the traverse didn't end when I arrived at my destination – I still had to endure medical tests to monitor the data. Speaking to the team and my mother, I couldn't believe that I had already climbed forty-eight 4,000-metre peaks since the start of the adventure.

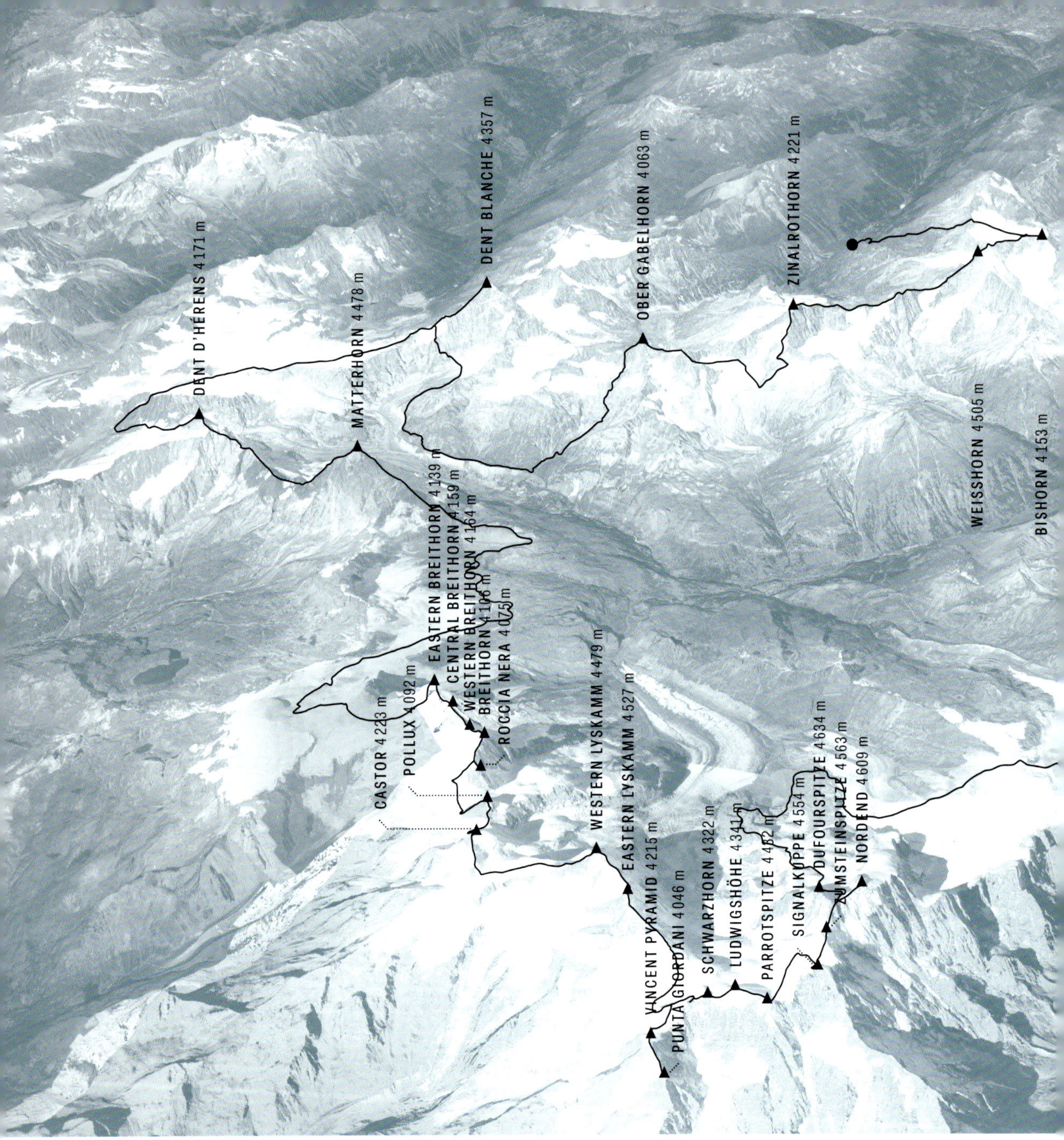

STAGES:
4–9

CLIMBING
BIKING

TOTAL PEAKS > 4,000 m (13,123 ft):
38

TOTAL ELEVATION GAIN:
26,372 m/86,522 ft

TOTAL DISTANCE:
221 km/137 miles

TOTAL SLEEP:
29:00:00

TOTAL ACTIVITY:
93:06:45

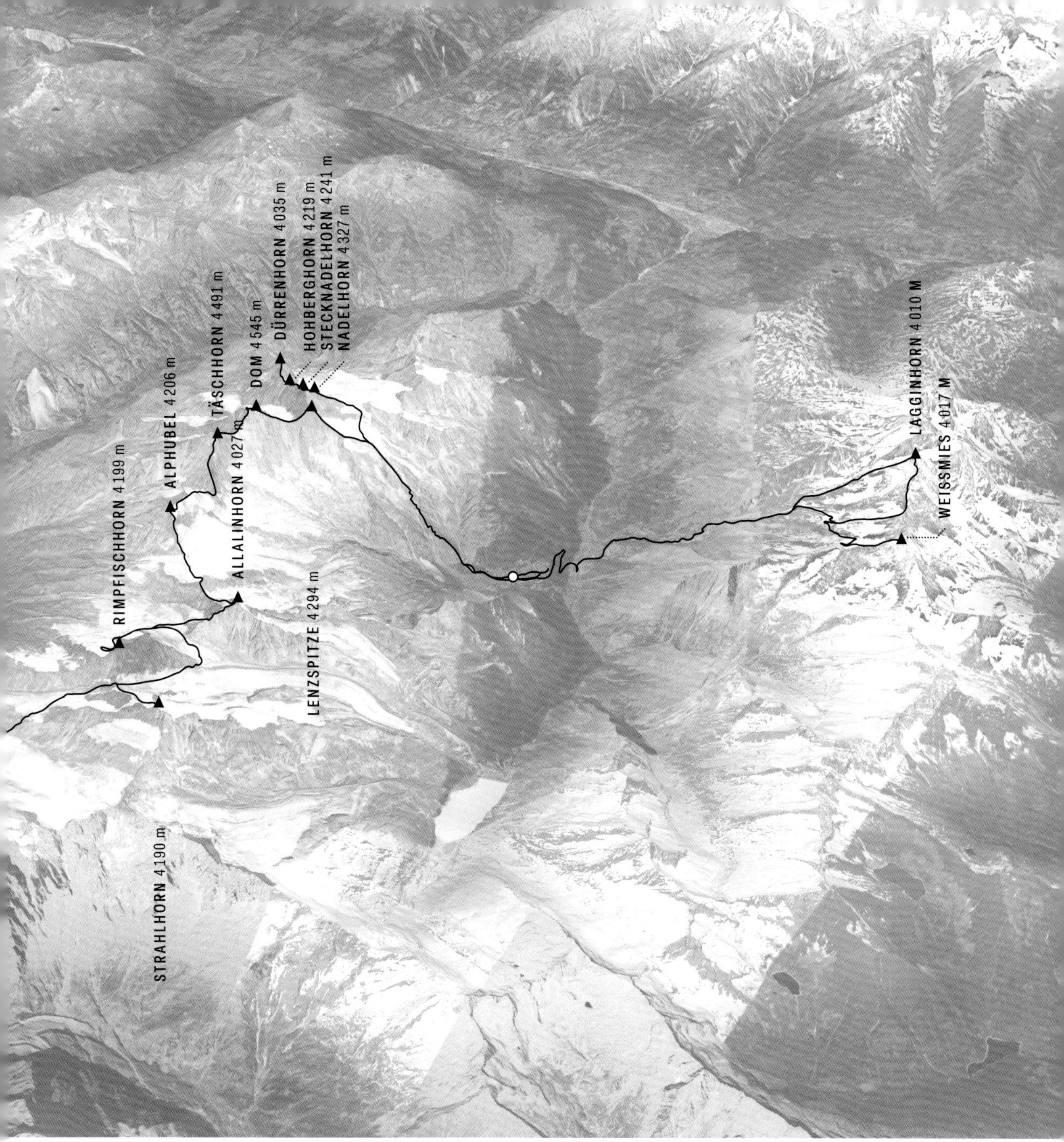
RIMPFISCHHORN 4 199 m
ALPHUBEL 4 206 m
TÄSCHHORN 4 491 m
DOM 4 545 m
DÜRRENHORN 4 035 m
HOHBERGHORN 4 219 m
STECKNADELHORN 4 241 m
NADELHORN 4 327 m
ALLALINHORN 4 027 m
LENZSPITZE 4 294 m
STRAHLHORN 4 190 m
LAGGINHORN 4 010 M
WEISSMIES 4 017 M

ELEVATION:

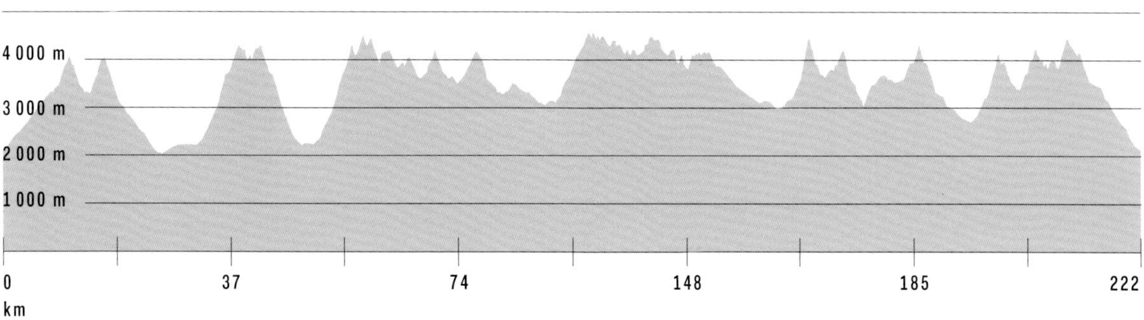
4 000 m
3 000 m
2 000 m
1 000 m
0
37
74
148
185
222
km

THE MOUNTAIN, DAY AFTER DAY

STAGES:
10–11

49.	COMBIN DE VALSOREY	4184 m
50.	COMBIN DE GRAFENEIRE	4314 m
51.	COMBIN DE LA TSESSETTE	4135 m

It had been ten days since I started to traverse my beloved Alpine summits, and each day had been different. This was an enriching experience, one that constantly put me to the test. The effort piled up with each climb, and I kept a close eye on my body day after day: its constants, its reactions, its ways of adapting. After all, this analysis also formed part of the challenge.

That day, 23 August, for the first time I was able to sleep peacefully and for a longer period of time: five hours straight, no more no less. I think I deserved it. I understand how these words may come as a surprise to people who are used to other sleep schedules, but as an athlete, and considering the journey I'm on, it seemed almost excessive.

When I got up, I picked up my bike with the intention of relaxing my body a little, and I descended by a route that I had taken many times. The last time, in fact, was just over a week before on a bus heading to the start of the Sierre-Zinal. I went at a snail's pace, enjoying every stride until I reached Martigny. It was like being on a hike, no competitive pressure. It wasn't about the urgency anymore, but rather the pleasure of taking in the magnificent countryside views at a slower pace. As I was going down, I was feeling like a battery recharging: my body was clearly regaining the energy spent over the previous days.

I arrived in Bourg-Saint-Pierre, a small town in the Swiss Valais with barely 200 residents. It's a town like any other but seeing it there in front of me made me smile. I got off my bike and I immediately appreciated how cycling had been beneficial to my body. It was such a joy to catch up with my team too; they had arrived ahead of me and welcomed me with the warmth only true friends can provide. To top it all off, there was also a very special guest: Alan Tissières.

Alan and I met when he started doing ski mountaineering, 'skimo' for short. He was quite young when we met, but he already stood out for his physical abilities and his incredible talent. I've experienced unforgettable moments with him – and this may seem trivial, but the first ones that come to mind are the post-race parties and celebrations, which are always highly appreciated and a great deal of fun.

That morning, Alan had been working as a guide on Dent Blanche, an iconic mountain in the Pennine Alps, known for its nearly perfect pyramid-shaped outline. Despite its name, it's not part of the Mont Blanc massif, but it rises in the Valais, majestic and solitary. Due to its shape, it's sometimes confused with the Matterhorn, but it is more technical and less visited. Now that he's a full-time guide, Alan often spends his time on

↑ 23.08.24/ZINAL
After a restorative five-hour sleep, I embark on stage 10, one of the most technical and high-risk stages on the entire traverse.

← P. 108
23.08.24/GRAND COMBIN
One constant was the joy of slowly contemplating the landscape, the magnificent view pulling me in like a magnet.

→ 23.08.24/ZINAL
I got on my bike to loosen up my body and rode 110 km (68 miles) to Bourg-Saint-Pierre.

↑ 29.08.24/VALSOREY MOUNTAIN HUT
A shared moment with Isabelle, the warden at the Valsorey hut and Alan's cousin, and one of my companions on this adventure.

the mountain, but knowing that I was coming, he decided to be my rope partner on 'his' mountain, the one he calls home, the Grand Combin. I sure am grateful he did. This massif is formed of three peaks: COMBIN DE VALSOREY (4,184 m/13,727 ft), COMBIN DE GRAFENEIRE (4,314 m/14,153 ft) and COMBIN DE LA TSESSETTE (4,135 m/13,566 ft). Alan has lived here all his life – and that's a privilege. Even though he has retired from competition, he is still in excellent physical shape, which is not so common.

Grand Combin, for all its majesty, remains a rather lonely mountain: mountaineers avoid it due to its famous 'Death Couloir', a segment prone to serac avalanches – giant towers of ice that fall from the Corbassière Glacier. This has earned it a fearful reputation, and even local guides limit ascents.

We set out along the trail feeling strong. Even though I had already travelled 100 kilometres (62 miles), I was well rested and in a good mood. The trail to the Valsorey mountain hut is simple, and we did it quickly. Alan's cousin, who is the hut's warden, welcomed us. She was a wonderful host, who gave us a very warm welcome – although she did tell us off for running without a helmet, which she thought imprudent. She still gave us water, thankfully! Alan argued that if there had been a rock slide the helmet wouldn't have helped us much anyway. She still wasn't convinced.

That evening, we continued our climb to the pass where the Meitin ridge starts. More than a ridge, it is a huge wall with a zig-zag trail. The rock is solid if you don't stray from the trail, but in quite a poor state if you do. And to be fair, it's quite easy to stray or even get lost there. The ascent isn't that steep: a section that can be easily walked, followed by a few metres/yards of climbing, and so on for half a kilometre (third of a mile).

When we arrived at the peak of Valsorey, we were greeted by what was turning out to be a familiar sight: an enchanting sunset. The sun was setting behind the Mont Blanc range, while a storm was illuminating the Italian high plateau.

From the peak, we took out the rope and the headlamps to continue along the snowy ridge to the Grand Combin, passing by the Aiguille du Croissant and the Combin de la Tsessette, before returning, cutting below the Grand Combin, to the first summit.

Back at the mountain hut, Alan surprised me with a couple of slices of cake. We savoured them with immense satisfaction, while also appreciating the silence of a starry night.

Alan stayed at the hut, while I continued on to the village. Before setting off, the hut wardens, who were getting ready to

← 23.08.24/BOURG-SAINT-PIERRE
In Bourg-Saint-Pierre I met up with Alan Tissières; we talked for a while about our lives and the mountains.

‘What impressed us the most was that he looked like he was simply out for a stroll, or doing a routine training session. He has an incredible level of mountaineering ability, physical strength and determination – but above all, he remains humble. He didn’t make a big deal out of the incredible challenge he was undertaking. It says a lot about him.’

SABRINA BENDOTTI

Sabrina Bendotti is the manager of the Margherita Mountain Hut (4,554 m/14,941 ft). She was there the day Kilian dropped by. She is also a mountain runner and a mountaineer.

↑ 23.08.24/MEITIN ARÊTE
Despite its majesty, the Grand Combin is a solitary mountain: many mountaineers avoid it because of its notorious Death Couloir.

← 23.08.24/MEITIN ARÊTE
The ascent to the Grand Combin is beautiful but perilous, with rockfall and challenging route-finding.

↑ 23.08.24/MEITIN ARÊTE
Another breathtaking view: the golden glow of sunset at Mont Vélan.

← 23.08.24/COL DU MEITIN
With the sun setting, we started the ascent of the Combin de Valsorey.

sleep outside, gave me great encouragement and wished me luck.

It had been a long stage – 134 kilometres (83 miles) in fact – combining cycling and climbing, with fourteen hours of activity on the Grand Combin. It was more technical than I had expected, but it offered an incredible climb. The mountain's inherent danger has made it one of the least-frequented four-thousanders in the Alps. For all these reasons, I am very happy to have shared it with Alan and that we both got out of it unscathed!

The next day, the eleventh stage was relatively easy, almost like a transition. I arrived in Bourg-Saint-Pierre at two in the morning, hopped on my bike to cycle the 30 kilometres (18.6 miles) to La Fouly, still on Swiss ground.

There, I had the pleasure to bump into Jules-Henri Gabioud, the ultramarathon runner, who was undertaking his final training session before competing in the PTL, the Petite Trotte à Léon. This ultra-endurance event around Mont Blanc is known for its incredible spirit: mental commitment, teamwork, adventure and defending mountain values. It is an example of best practices: we are people with a firm commitment to our planet, not record-beating machines.

It was in fact Jules-Henri who found me, overtaking me on his bike. We rode the last kilometre until La Fouly together. Jules-Henri kindly and rightly suggested that I climb along the Petit Col Ferret to cross over into Italy, in order to avoid the Grand Col, which would soon be packed with people running in the legendary race. This small mountain pass, which connects the Swiss Val Ferret with the Italian one, is one of the calmer sections of the Tour du Mont Blanc. For centuries, it was used by local smugglers who knew these border valleys inside out. I took his advice and we parted ways. I wished him luck on the PTL.

I left my bike and ran towards the Italian side of Val Ferret, to the Jorasses campsite, where the team was waiting for me. Once there, I ate, rested, then checked the weather forecast. It was terrible: a severe thunderstorm and heavy snowfall.

The next stage was a demanding one, both physically and technically, and I seriously considered taking a break. It wasn't part of the plan, but that was okay. Setting off in bad weather could make the ascent dangerous and I needed to be careful. Sometimes you need to know when to stop. This was one of those times.

So, after a brief internal debate, I decided to take a day of rest. I would wait until midnight, at a time when a more favourable weather window was forecast. Up till then, I would get some proper rest: eat heartily to regain my strength, drink a lot of water to stay hydrated and treat the injuries on my hands and feet. I would also carefully prepare for the next stage of the *Alpine Connections* project – a very technical one.

↑ 24.08.24/BOURG-SAINT-PIERRE
After the Grand Combin, I needed to find my balance again with a 30-km (18.6-mile) stage on the bike to reach La Fouly.

↑→ 24.08.24/JORASSES CAMPSITE
The conditions on the mountains weren't good, so I decided to take a rest day waiting for them to improve before taking on a key part of the traverse. So far, fifty-one summits climbed.

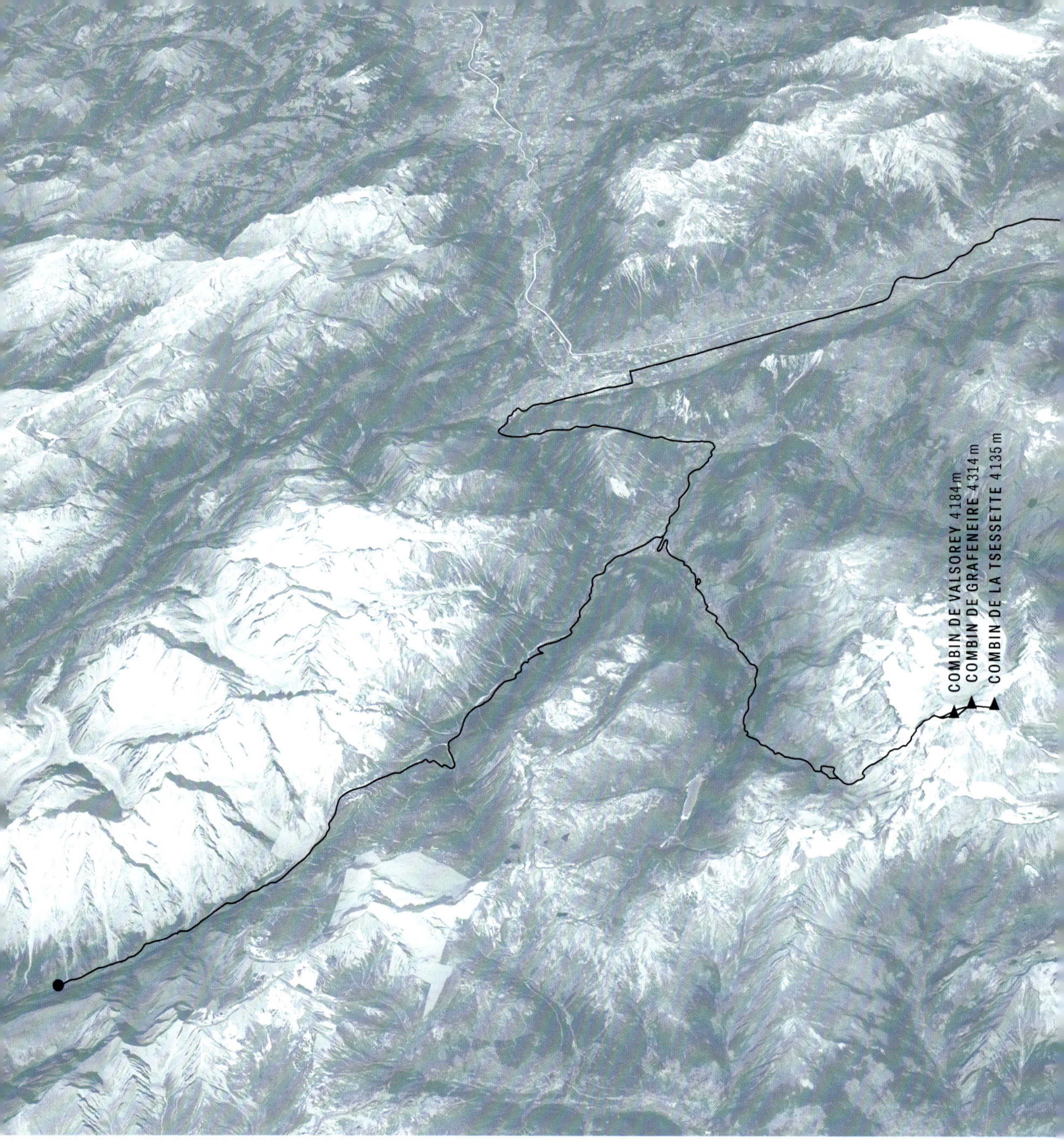

STAGES:
10–11

CLIMBING
BIKING
TRAIL RUNNING

TOTAL PEAKS > 4,000 m (13,123 ft):
3

TOTAL ELEVATION GAIN:
5,835 m/19,144 ft

TOTAL ACTIVITY:
178.96 km/111.2 miles

TOTAL SLEEP:
08:00:00

TOTAL ACTIVITY:
17:47:28

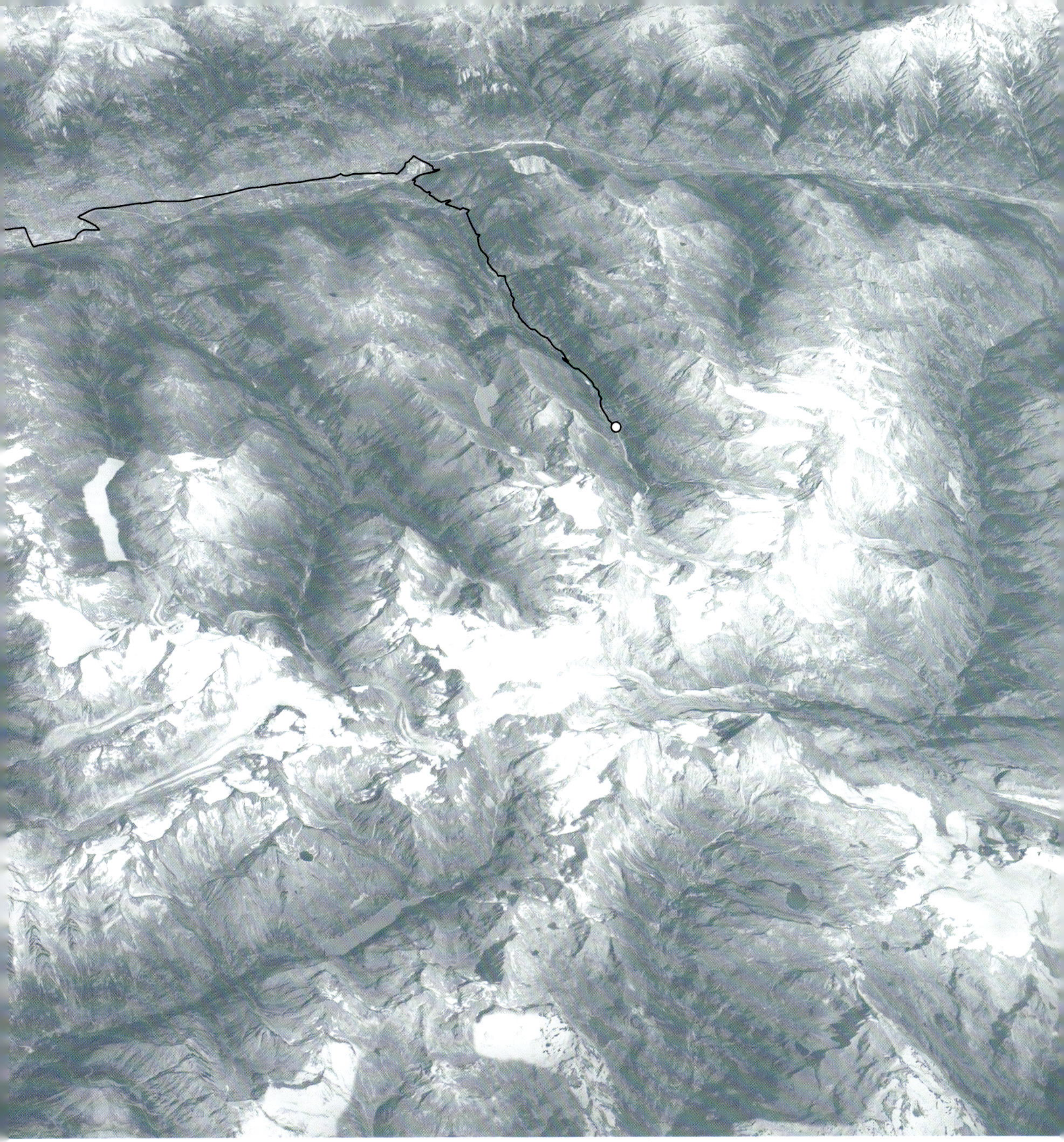

ELEVATION:

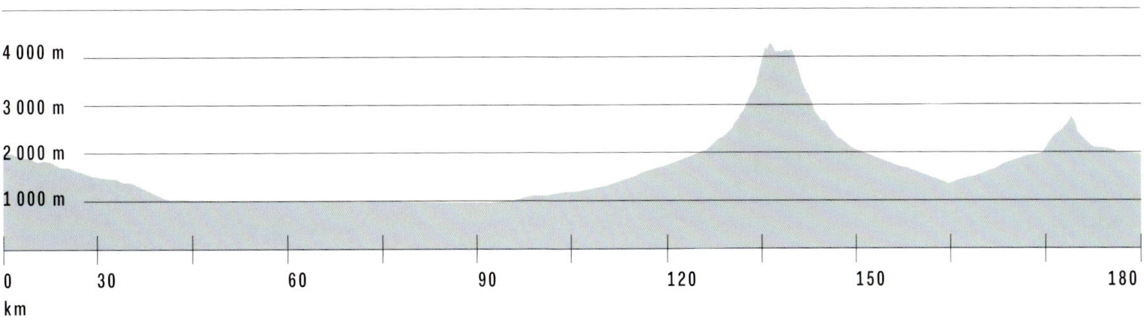

Norwal

EACH SUMMIT, A DEEPER CONNECTION WITH MYSELF

STAGE:
12

52.	POINTE WALKER	4 208 m
53.	POINTE WHYMPER	4 184 m
54.	POINTE CROZ	4 110 m
55.	POINTE ELENA	4 045 m
56.	POINTE MARGUERITE	4 065 m
57.	DÔME DE ROCHEFORT	4 015 m
58.	AIGUILLE DE ROCHEFORT	4 001 m
59.	DENT DU GÉANT	4 013 m

125

The rest from the previous day had done me a world of good. The twelve days' worth of mileage and elevation gain were starting to take their toll on me. And not just physically.

We usually measure the distances we cover in numbers, and we have objective, highly precise metrics to record them – altitude, distance, time – as well as formulas that reflect the state of our bodies. We can turn them into a series of graphs that tell us about performance, fatigue, recovery, sleep quality and dozens of other variables, supposedly giving a perfectly clear and detailed picture of what we feel, down to the slightest beat of our smallest cells.

All that said, during those days spent linking the four-thousanders in the Alps, each time I reached a peak or climbed a ridge, there was a particular moment – recurring yet always unique – that felt truly extraordinary. This moment was when I sat down, once the goal was reached. I looked behind me, ahead, up and all around me. I was then overwhelmed by a flood of emotions and sensations of every kind.

How can we measure what we're feeling in a graph? I've thought about this my whole life. Is there anyone, in some hidden laboratory in a remote building, who can show me and others a statistic or a diagram, which objectively portrays the feelings that hit me after an exhausting day, full of challenges that I have overcome and dangers that I've managed to avoid? Would they be capable of entering units and tenths into a spreadsheet cell corresponding to the contemplation of the sun slipping through thick clouds, sending down to me a light that cuts through the darkness stretching as far as the eye can see? Or when I lean on a rock ledge looking out towards the horizon and I'm filled with awe by the majesty of a landscape devoid of any human presence?

On these occasions I'm overwhelmed by all sorts of feelings. It's difficult to put it into words, but what I'm feeling is very intense, very real. It's a deep connection between my mind and the mountains that I'm climbing, felt with my entire being.

And during these musings of mine, I always reach the same clarity and certainty: technical difficulties aside, it's always important to keep in mind the mental context of those moments when I take on the mountain. I am doing this on my own most of the time, sometimes accompanied.

It's with this mindset that I got up, very early. I had a special day ahead of me. Not only due to the route ahead, but also because I wasn't going to do it on my own. It was a festive day in

← P. 124
26.08.24 / AIGUILLE DE ROCHEFORT
Looking back and seeing myself holding on to the only fixed rope in the entire project, I'm proud of what I've done, though it will take some time for me to truly fully comprehend.

→ 26.08.24 / COURMAYEUR
Feeling fit and rested, I left our campsite at midnight to start the ascent of the Grandes Jorasses, accompanied by a great team: Mathéo, Michel Lanne and Bastien Lardat.

Courmayeur, but for me the real reason for joy was to resume the climb – and to do so with company. Joining me were old friends with whom I had shared many mountain adventures: Mathéo of course, and also Michel Lanne, an old race partner now member of the PGHM, the French high mountain gendarme corps. He brought another friend with him, his colleague Bastien Lardat, also from the same corps. It was a mixed group, but we had a good team spirit, full of anticipation to share the trail.

The target for the day was nothing short of majestic. We were going to cross the Grandes Jorasses, a rocky snow-lined ridge that marks the border between France and Italy. It's a legendary name in the history of mountaineering, a mountain that impresses the moment it appears against the sky.

From Val Ferret, we started the ascent towards the Boccalatte hut. We were climbing at a lively, but comfortable, speed. It was night, yet the sky was still clear and the conditions were ideal – compact snow, dry air – so we reached the peak of POINTE WALKER (4,208 m/13,806 ft) at a swift pace. We arrived before sunrise, when temperatures were still bitterly cold. We didn't linger, and headed westwards.

It was the second time I was crossing the Jorasses, but the first in this direction. I thought that it would be less spectacular than the previous one, perhaps because I already knew what awaited me. But I was wrong: it was just as impressive, if not more so. The itinerary was surprisingly fluid, with less rappelling than I had expected, and an elegant climbing line on high-quality rock. Michel and Bastien, with their local expertise, chose a route that struck me as visually pleasing and logical.

We moved onwards at a lively pace. The expansive, airy ridge offered breathtaking views. The relief of the north face of the Jorasses – that legendary wall of rock and ice – was intimidating and fascinating in equal measure. It felt like we were treading the path of mountaineering history: POINTE WHYMPER (4,184 m/13,727 ft), summited for the first time on 24 June 1865 by Edward Whymper, Christian Almer and Franz Biner; Pointe Walker, climbed by Horace Walker and his team three years later; and POINTE CROZ (4,110 m/13,484 ft), POINTE ELENA (4,045 m/13,271 ft), POINTE MARGUERITE (4,065 m/13,337 ft) and POINTE YOUNG (3,996 m/13,110 ft), whose names are reminders of the feats and epic adventures of these mountaineering pioneers.

The day was moving ahead, but the cold remained. We couldn't slow down much, but the surroundings made up for it. The sun finally showed up right at Pointe Young, like a

↑ 26.08.24/COURMAYEUR
Everyone was excited to be there and set off in such great company. They all knew the area well and I was grateful to have them along for the more technical climbs.

↑ 26.08.24/ROCHEFORT
The Grandes Jorasses is a legendary name in the history of mountaineering, a mountain that impresses the moment it appears against the sky.

→ PP. 130–131
26.08.24/ROCHEFORT
We didn't know what to expect during the climb, but with ropes and the proper gear we were prepared for everything.

tender embrace. The warm rays revived us, and we continued on towards the DÔME DE ROCHEFORT (4,015 m/13,173 ft), followed by the AIGUILLE DE ROCHEFORT (4,001 m/13,127 ft) and the DENT DU GÉANT (4,013 m/13,166 ft).

At which point we went our separate ways. Michel and Bastien chose to descend directly to the Turin mountain hut, where we would reunite with them at the end of the day. For the next leg, we were joined by Noa. And with Mathéo, the three of us decided to climb the summit.

The Dent du Géant is truly spectacular with its impressive crowning granite monolith. From a distance, on the horizon of the Mont Blanc range, it looks almost like a sculpture. If it had been carved by an artist, it wouldn't look out of place in an art gallery. It's an iconic summit, with some of the best granite imaginable – it even has its own name in this area, 'protagine', and is more or less transformed with a greenish appearance.

Sadly one detail spoils the overall beauty, foreign to the monolith. And it's no surprise that it is a direct consequence of human activity. Despite the number of cracks in the wall,

there are numerous fixed ropes, which not only ruin the view but also take away the sense of facing a real mountaineering challenge.

Once at the summit, we descended quickly in the direction of the Turin mountain hut. We ate a bit, drank and we rested. I decided to call Tom Lafaille for advice. Just one week earlier, he had descended along the Mer de Glace, and I asked him what conditions he'd experienced when crossing the glacier. Tom is the son of a mountaineering legend, Jean-Christophe Lafaille, who lost his life in 2006 in Makalu, Nepal. It's hard to come to terms with such a painful loss, and my friend Tom chose, as a way of coping, to follow in his father's footsteps.

Mathéo, Michel, Bastien and Noa stayed on in the Turin hut, and I descended by the Vallée Blanche towards the Requin hut. Along the way, I had to use my crampons to get through some delicate passes and crevasses and cut straight into this expanse of ice. I arrived with enough daylight to enjoy the mountain hut, a rare feat indeed. What's more, I managed to have a leisurely meal, sitting down and having a chat with fellow mountaineers

↑ 26.08.24/ROCHEFORT ARÊTE
Up there, at midpoint in the traverse, I felt small, overwhelmed by so much majesty, but overflowing with happiness.

→ 26.08.24/DENT DU GÉANT
The Dent du Géant looks almost like a sculpture. With its impressive crowning granite monolith, it is simply spectacular.

‘What I’ll remember the most is the boldness and adaptability shown throughout this Alpine adventure. You need to have lived it to understand it and coming down from these mountains will surely take some time.’

MATHÉO JACQUEMOUD

Mathéo Jacquemoud is an athlete and mountain guide. He’s a great friend of Kilian and has shared many sporting experiences with him.

↑ 26.08.24 / TURIN MOUNTAIN HUT
We grabbed a little food and drink at the mountain hut. We rested a while and talked about just how beautiful the stage that we had finished truly was.

and the hut wardens. A luxury I hadn't been able to afford much during this expedition.

From the terrace, the view stretched out beautifully: the Mer de Glace below, the Jorasses ridge to the right, Mont Blanc towering over everything on the other side. I felt small, yet happy.

One more surprise was waiting for me at the hut: my friend Simón Elías, a mountaineer and author from La Rioja in Spain. We had climbed the Colton-MacIntyre together in 2015. He now lives in Chamonix – to search for Yeti, the Abominable Snowman – he jokes. Just like everyone else! In reality, he works as a guide and he spends his summers looking for rock crystals, which takes him to visit the most weathered walls of the mountain range, where these precious metals form. We discussed the following day. The mountain, he warned, was changing rapidly. Certain parts were crumbling, and we would need to be very careful. In order to minimize the risks, we considered alternative routes to come up with the best one.

Once I was alone, I replayed the day in my mind. The stage had been complicated, and highly technical. I had managed to summit eight four-thousanders over a period of eighteen hours. In total, I had covered 28 kilometres (17.4 miles). It was a day well spent. And now, another formidable challenge presented itself: the Mont Blanc massif. I had to carefully gauge my physical and psychological capacities to truly connect with all the legendary spaces that awaited me.

← PP. 134–138
26.08.24/DENT DU GÉANT
It was my second crossing of the Jorasses and this time around, the route was surprisingly smooth, with less rappelling than I had expected, and an elegant climbing line on high-quality rock.

→ PP. 140–141
26.08.24/GRANDES JORASSES
The sunsets painted the sky with orange light, bathing the wild landscape in a serene elegance.

STAGE:
12

CLIMBING

TOTAL PEAKS > 4,000 m (13,123 ft):
8

TOTAL ELEVATION GAIN:
4,199 m/13,776 ft

TOTAL DISTANCE:
28.29 km (17.6 miles)

TOTAL SLEEP:
05:00:00

TOTAL ACTIVITY:
18:22:34

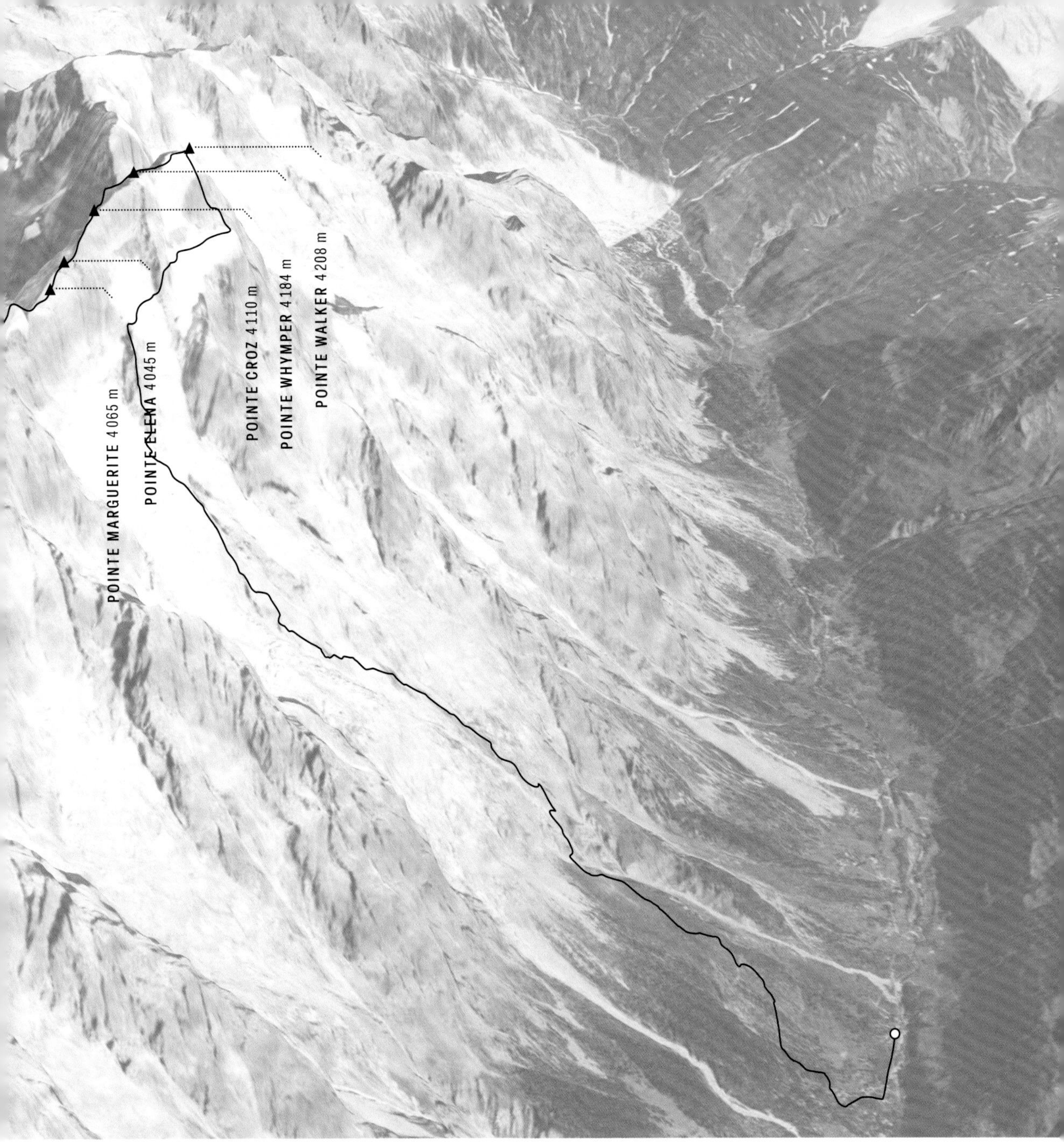
POINTE MARGUERITE 4065 m
POINTE ELENA 4045 m
POINTE CROZ 4110 m
POINTE WHYMPER 4184 m
POINTE WALKER 4208 m

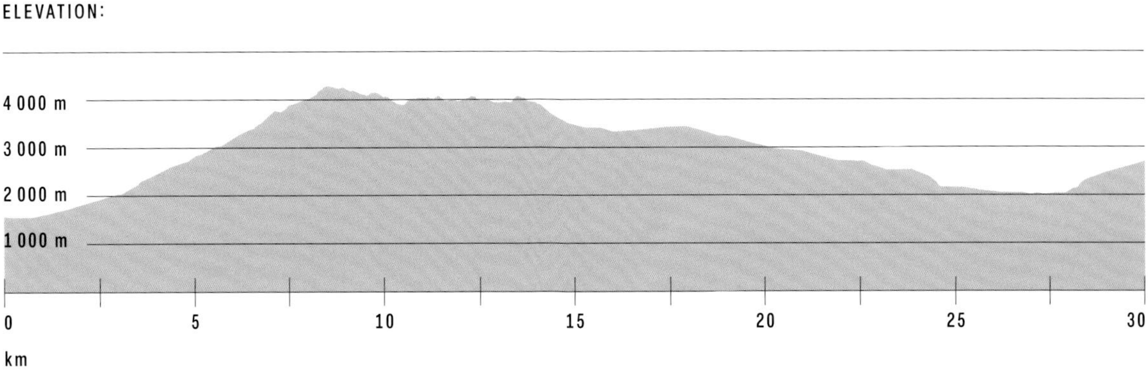
ELEVATION:
4 000 m
3 000 m
2 000 m
1 000 m
0
5
10
15
20
25
30
km

THE RHYTHM OF THE MOUNTAIN

STAGES:
13-14

60.	AIGUILLE VERTE	4122 m
61.	GRANDE ROCHEUSE	4102 m
62.	AIGUILLE DU JARDIN	4035 m
63.	LES DROITES	4000 m
64.	CORNE DU DIABLE	4064 m
65.	POINTE CHAUBERT	4074 m
66.	POINTE MÉDIANE	4097 m
67.	POINTE CARMEN	4109 m
68.	L'ISOLÉE	4114 m
69.	MONT BLANC DU TACUL	4248 m
70.	MONT MAUDIT	4465 m
71.	MONT BLANC	4809 m
72.	DÔME DU GOÛTER	4304 m
73.	AIGUILLE DE BIONNASSAY	4052 m
74.	MONT BLANC DE COURMAYEUR	4748 m
75.	PIC LUIGI AMEDEO	4469 m
76.	MONT BROUILLARD	4069 m
77.	PUNTA BARETTI	4013 m
78.	GRAND PILIER D'ANGLE	4243 m
79.	AIGUILLE BLANCHE DE PEUTEREY	4112 m

The thirteenth stage started at four in the morning on 27 August. After having breakfast, I started the ascent of MONT BLANC, the highest peak in the Alps, towering at 4,809 metres (15,778 feet). Although I was in good spirits and feeling strong physically, I was aware that my body was tired and the day ahead would bring great risks. Before dawn, I crossed the *bergschrund* (deep crevasse) and started the ascent of the Arête du Moine towards the AIGUILLE VERTE (4,122 m/13,524 ft). The ridge I knew was no more; it had become a very unstable route due to numerous landslides, and its shape had completely changed.

I made my way to the Aiguille Verte summit, a route I knew well after having skied there that very winter. Now, in summer, there was no covering of ice and snow hiding the rock. In these conditions, the summit is spectacular. It is slightly set apart from the main massif and offers a unique view, with the north face of the Grandes Jorasses ahead, the Argentière Basin on one side, and the Mer de Glace with the Aiguilles de Chamonix and Mont Blanc on the other. There aren't many easy routes to reach the summit. I was reminded of the wise words of legendary mountaineer Gaston Rébuffat: 'Before the Verte you're an alpinist; after the Verte, you're a mountaineer'.

From the summit, I followed a narrow snowy ridge that led me to the top of the GRANDE ROCHEUSE (4,102 m/13,458 ft). It was exactly then, as I was climbing and descending the AIGUILLE DU JARDIN (4,035 m/13,238 ft), that the danger that would come to characterize the entire day started to make itself felt. If I stayed on the ridge, the rock held together reasonably well, but as soon as I had to move to one side or the other, I felt like I was playing Jenga, where you have to pull out pieces one by one without the whole thing collapsing. The Aiguille du Jardin certainly offers magnificent views, but my mind was focused on how to descend the safest way possible. My concerns proved well-founded; it was a terrible descent. I made a few rappels in very precarious conditions. A large part of this wall had collapsed not long before. I could even see the permafrost exposed to the sun, with large intact blocks the size of a car. I upped the pace so as not to stay exposed for too long. To the right, huge boulders would occasionally collapse, triggering large rockfalls. All in all, it was very scary.

I finally arrived at the Col de la Verte. Along the way I grew a few grey hairs from all the scares I had. The rock there wasn't any more solid, but on the bright side I was on the ridge, so at least nothing could fall on my head.

↑ 27.08.24/COUVERCLE MOUNTAIN HUT

In the fog, the start of one of the most iconic and demanding stages of the route: Mont Blanc.

← P. 144

29.08.24/MONT BLANC DU TACUL

The moon was a faithful companion throughout the traverse, guiding my way on several occasions.

↑ 27.08.24/ARÊTE DU MOINE
The route to Aiguille Verte was quite unstable, strewn with countless rockfalls, but the views were stunning, with a perspective unlike any other.

I descended as quickly as I could to the south until I found myself facing LES DROITES. At precisely 4,000 metres (13,123 feet) high, this peak only just makes the list of four-thousanders in the Alps. I tried to stay on the ridge, but sometimes I had to go around a gendarme on one side or the other. And that's when one of those events that make your blood run cold occurred: suddenly all the rocks I was holding onto with my feet and one hand came loose from the wall and fell all the way down to the Argentière Glacier, a few hundred metres below. Luckily, I still had a firm grip with the other hand, and I stayed there, suspended in a precarious balance, praying that the rock I was holding onto would stay put, even if just for a moment.

If I can acknowledge one quality in myself, it's that I don't get too stressed. I'm quite lucky in this regard and, very often, it gives me the edge, when I'm competing or undertaking projects like this one, where concentration and calm are key factors. That said, I have no trouble admitting that it's one of the rare occasions when my stomach was so tight it actually hurt – and that lasted for hours. Truth be told, I didn't know if I'd make it. When

← **27.08.24/AIGUILLE DU JARDIN**
The descent was extremely complex, even precarious: the face had collapsed, the permafrost was exposed, and there were rock avalanches.

I reached the peak of Les Droites, I didn't pause to enjoy the landscape. I wanted to descend as quickly as possible. It seemed that there was snow at the Col des Droites and that the path was safer, but the gully to reach it was a bowl-shaped depression. I opted to downclimb the spur and cross towards the snowy fields. After a few hundred metres/yards I found a path to cross the depression and finally reach the snow. It was the first time in hours that I felt safe.

During the descent and traverse to the Couvercle hut, I wasn't sure what state of mind I was in. It was a strange sensation; I didn't feel right in myself. I was angry at myself for making the call to keep going earlier in the day. The small decisions I'd made – where to rappel, which way to go, how to descend, how to protect myself – had been the right ones, and that's why I was still alive. But the choice to keep going when I was at the first summit had been the wrong call, and I don't feel proud of it. The mountain had sent me a warning, and I ignored it. This time, I had been forgiven, but I realize now that I was playing Russian roulette that day. Push your luck too much, and it will run out...

I reached the hut exhausted, especially mentally. I had a brief chat with the hut warden and ate. I then returned to the Mer de Glace and followed my tracks from the previous day back up to the Turin hut. It started to rain and it was already dark when I reached the hut. Waiting for me there were Jordi Tosas, a good friend who works as a guide, as well as Mathéo,

THE MOUNTAIN COMMANDS

The mountain is an excellent teacher: it warns you of dangers, allows you to learn, offers challenges along the journey of learning, shows you your mistakes and successes and, above all, reconciles you with yourself – with who you truly are, at your core.

High in the mountains, no matter how long you've been there or how much experience you've gained, each day is different. It is the mountain that sets the pace, and you must adapt your body and mind to its rhythm, for you know full well that it is always the mountain that commands. Always.

You can plan, prepare or try to anticipate the challenges it will present; you can reason based on strict logic – but it is the mountain that will determine your path, with its seductive power and the questions it forces you to ask yourself.

Maybe that's why I love it so much.

While preparing for this project, with the goal of stringing together these Alpine routes, I devised a plan to link the summits via ridges and logical paths. All this pre-planning required a tremendous amount of work: I was unfamiliar with some areas, others involved routes for which I could find no information, and for some, like Mont Blanc, plotting a logical and feasible route seemed impossible. But, once I was on the ground, even if it looked like I had everything under control, I was forced to make amendments. Like I said: the mountain commands and puts us in our place.

I saw the clearest evidence of this in Mont Blanc.

↑ 27.08.24/AIGUILLE VERTE – LES DROITES
Instability was a constant throughout the traverse. I even found myself praying that the wall would hold as I was clinging to the rock with only one hand.

‘When he arrives and starts eating while recounting all the adventures of his day, without showing any concern for the fatigue he should be feeling, he is incredible.’

AINA GARCÍA

Aina García is a member of Kilian’s team. She is in charge of the project’s logistics.

Noa, Aina and my mum. We enjoyed a delicious, hearty meal, and I slept well, trying to clear my mind.

The next day, Jordi spent a moment with us at breakfast before heading to the hut to return to his clients. Mathéo and I resumed the traverse in silence, along the glacier surrounding the Grand Capucin, still shrouded in darkness. When we turned a corner, we saw Noa's headlamp: he was already filming us.

The *bergschrund* to climb to the Col du Diable was quite steep. We improvised a foothold with an ice screw and a sling, and we shared a second ice axe between us to climb the 5 metres (16 feet) of sheer ice. Once at the top, we continued to make our way over fairly crumbly rock, even though it felt like marble to us compared to the day before. Then the sun rose, with a jaw-dropping show of light and colour.

While Mathéo started his ascent of POINTE CHAUBERT (4,074 m/13,366 ft), I made a quick round trip to the CORNE DU DIABLE (4,064 m/13,333 ft). We then continued together along this magnificent ridge, one of the most beautiful climbs in the region. We advanced at a good pace, savouring every moment.

↑ 27.08.24 / TURIN MOUNTAIN HUT
When I returned to the Turin hut, I was exhausted, especially mentally, and carried a lot of built-up tension. I was grateful to those who accompanied me.

↑ 28.08.24/AIGUILLE DU MIDI
I turn back and see the majesty of the mountains we've climbed, turning our existence into an extraordinary experience.

↑ 28.08.24/GRAND CAPUCIN
The second stage of Mont Blanc started before daybreak, in total darkness.

Six hours after having left the hut, we reached the peak of MONT BLANC DU TACUL (4,248 m/13,937 ft). David and Nick were waiting for us; they had climbed up ahead of us in order to film our arrival. After a quick chat, we set out again towards MONT MAUDIT (4,465 m/14,649 ft), the 'cursed mountain': a name rooted in tradition and the rather eerie legends of these mountains.

We found ourselves alone at the summit of Mont Blanc. It's a mountain which I hold dear – I lived at its foot for many years, and I have climbed it dozens of times: skiing, running and climbing. Every time I reach the top, I have the same sensation of being like a bird, great and small at the same time. I left the rope and some warm clothes that might come in handy when I returned later on. We descended by the normal route until the DÔME DU GOÛTER (4,304 m/14,121 ft), then we tackled the AIGUILLE DE BIONNASSAY (4,052 m/13,294 ft). I was surprised to see sections of bare rock, where on my previous trips there had been a perfect, narrow, snow-covered ridge. All the same, it was still breathtakingly beautiful.

Mathéo and Noa started their descent while I turned around to make for Mont Blanc once again. It was a long ascent, nearly

←↑ 28.08.24/CORNE DU DIABLE
At times, the granite was excellent and the snow magnificent; this made for one of the most magical climbs that I have ever done, both technically and aesthetically.

→ PP. 158–159
28.08.24/MONT MAUDIT
The so-called 'cursed mountain' welcomed us with bright sunshine and covered with snow, which allowed us to run and take great pleasure in it.

→ PP. 160–161
28.08.24/MONT BLANC DU TACUL
The ascent to the top of Mont Blanc du Tacul took about six hours.

a kilometre (0.6 miles) vertically, but I was feeling good and I reached the summit with relative ease. I picked up the rope and my clothes, and I started to descend along the south face.

I could make out a few old tracks, which made me think that perhaps I would find some higher up to cross the glaciers. It wasn't long before I ran into a couple of mountaineers who confirmed that the terrain was quite dry. Good news: this allowed me to continue descending with greater confidence.

I reached PIC LUIGI AMEDEO (4,469 m/14,662 ft) and, shortly after, I took off my crampons. Although the ridge isn't overly technical, there are some class-four passes that can be tricky on the descent. I still took the time to admire the beautiful sunset.

I managed the descent to the Col Émile Rey (named after a 19th-century guide who is considered one of the pioneers of mountaineering in the Alps) without any problems, even though I had to rappel for a short section. Night had fallen. I took off my rucksack and, guided by my headlamp, I continued along the ridge until PUNTA BARETTI (4,013 m/13,166 ft) and then I made my way back. There were foggy patches at times, and so I had to activate

the GPS's trackback function to retrace my outward route to avoid getting lost.

Up to that point, everything had seemed surprisingly easy. Too easy in fact. As I was crossing the glacier on MONT BROUILLARD (4,069 m/13,350 ft), I heard rockfall, and when I started the ascent to Col d'Eccles, I came across a giant crevasse that cut through the entire glacier. I looked all around, but there was no easy way to cross it. Damn.

After a moment's hesitation, I decided to turn back and descend the Brouillard Glacier to make my way to the Eccles Bivouac along the normal route. But the glacier was in very poor condition, and I couldn't find any safe path.

Disappointed, I had no other option but to go up the Émile Rey again, descend via the full Brouillard route until I reached Val Vény, then, the following day, to ascend along the normal route, first towards Eccles and then up to Frêney. When I crossed the glacier on the way back to the Émile Rey couloir, I heard a massive rockfall at the summit – a mass of boulders crashing against the face, the roar of a mountain falling on top of me. I ran for cover, as best I could, into the open glacier. A few seconds later, in the beam of my headlamp, I could see rocks the size of basketballs flying through the air.

When it stopped, I was shrouded in a thick cloud of dust that only dissipated after ten minutes. I have to admit that this time I got out by the skin of my teeth. I couldn't continue along that route. I had no choice but to return to the main crevasse. I crossed it again and found a snow bridge to get to the other side. There, I scaled 5 metres (16 feet) of rock face with my ice axe in one hand and my ice screw in the other.

The ascent was slow but safe. After a lot of effort, I found a way to the Eccles Bivouac. When I got there, I felt utterly exhausted – physically and emotionally spent. So I decided to call it a day. The best decision I could take was to rest a little and wait until there was enough light to establish where the rocks were falling from before continuing.

I finished the little food and water I had left, took off my wet shoes and socks, and I snuggled up in the three blankets that were in the bivouac. Those three hours of sleep were glorious: I slept like a log.

When I woke up, I waited for the first light of day. I left the bivouac and climbed to Pic d'Eccles. At sunrise, I was treated to one of the most stunning views of my life: the light spreading over the Col de Peuterey, the two peaks I was about to climb, and beyond them, La Verte, Les Droites and the Dent du Géant.

← PP. 162–163
27.08.24/MONT BLANC
Reaching the summit of the great mountain of the Alps, I feel both tiny and immense at the same time.

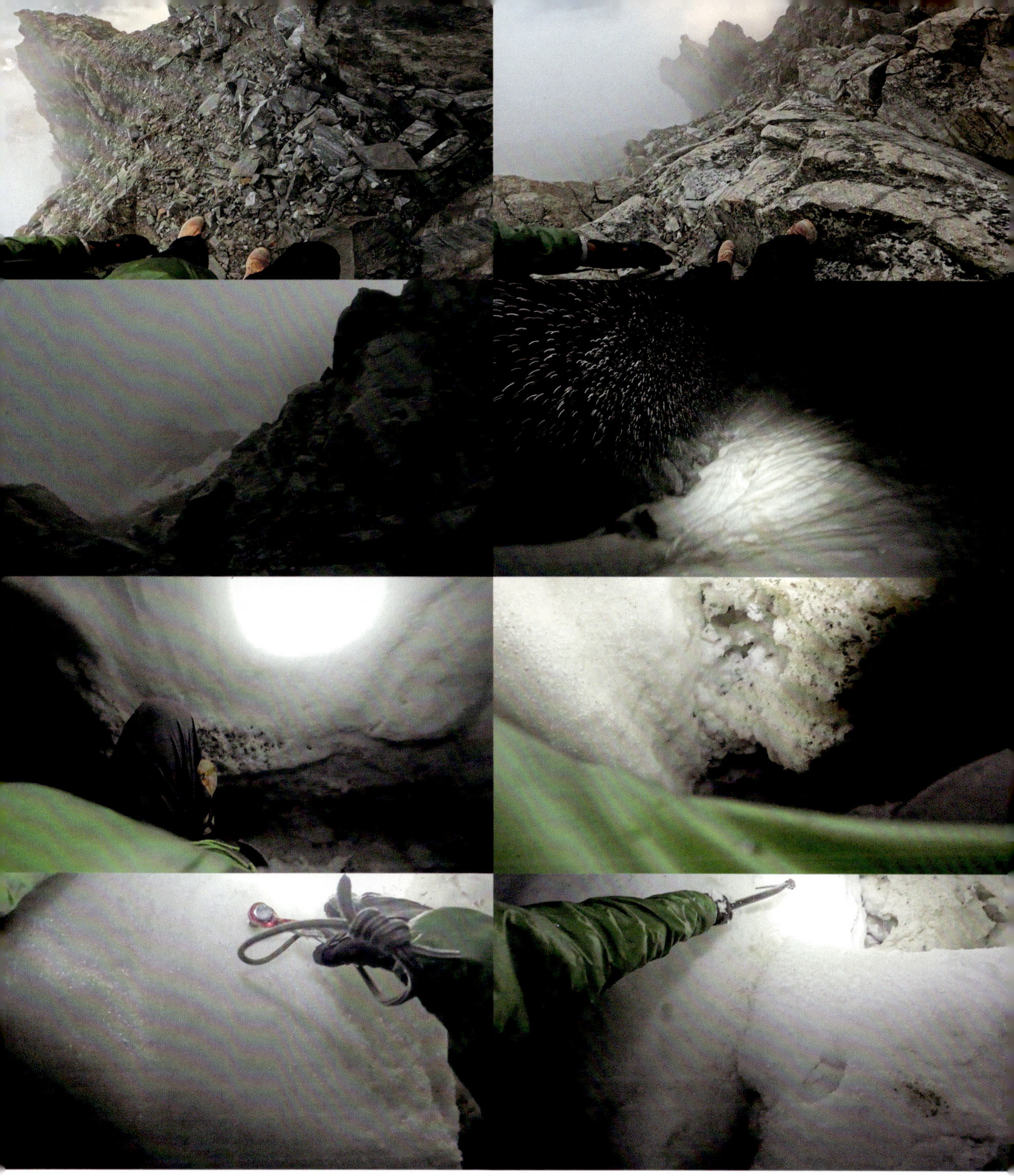

↑ **27.08.24/MONT BROUILLARD**
The end of the stage was complicated and exhausting: I had to readjust, double back and find a crevasse to get out.

←↑ 29.08.24/ECCLES BIVOUAC
The mountain demands patience, and that day I understood that taking a short break does not mean stopping, but moving forward sensibly, with self-care.

↑ 29.08.24/COL D'ECCLES
After a short break at the bivouac, I set off to tackle the last part of the Mont Blanc stage, greeted with one of the most splendid sunrises and views I had ever seen.

The Grandes Jorasses, which I had climbed only a few days prior, looked very far away from here.

My rope had been damaged by the falling rock from the previous days, so with the little rope I had left, I did a short rappel and descended via a dry gully until I reached the Frêney Glacier. The glacier presented perfect conditions: the snow was compact and no transverse crevasses. I reached Col du Peuterey in no time.

From there, I headed off to the GRAND PILIER D'ANGLE (4,243 m/13,921 ft), staying well to the right to avoid the constant rockfall in the central part. The climb proved more technical, but also safer.

I finally made it to the summit, where I found bits of old rope and took them with me to use for the rappels on the AIGUILLE BLANCHE DE PEUTEREY (4,112 m/13,491 ft). On the way down to the col, I left a rope to get across the *bergschrund* and then ascended the Aiguille Blanche, one of the most beautiful peaks in the region. I saw a rope team coming from the south, probably making the traverse from Peuterey.

↑ 29.08.24/FRÊNEY GLACIER
With little rope, but perfect conditions, I tackled the technical sections of the Grand Pilier d'Angle and the Aiguille Blanche de Peuterey.

→ 29.08.24/VALLON DE VALSOREY
Linking all the summits of Mont Blanc was an enormous challenge, but the experience surpassed all my expectations.

I stayed up at the summit for a while, savouring the opportunity to be there, at one with myself and with what I was doing. I did the descent with the short ropes. At the Monzino hut, I was finally able to eat and drink. I hadn't had anything for more than ten hours. I set off and made my way as quickly as I could towards La Sorgente campsite, where Matteo Pellin and his family gave me a warm welcome.

With the whole team assembled, it felt like the project's difficulties were now behind me. From this point on, I believed that climbing the last three peaks would only be a matter of physical effort. I got some good rest, took a shower and ate a lot to replenish both body and mind.

↑→ 30.08.24/LA SORGENTE CAMPSITE
The emotion was so intense in Mont Blanc that I wanted to capture it, in both sensation and image.

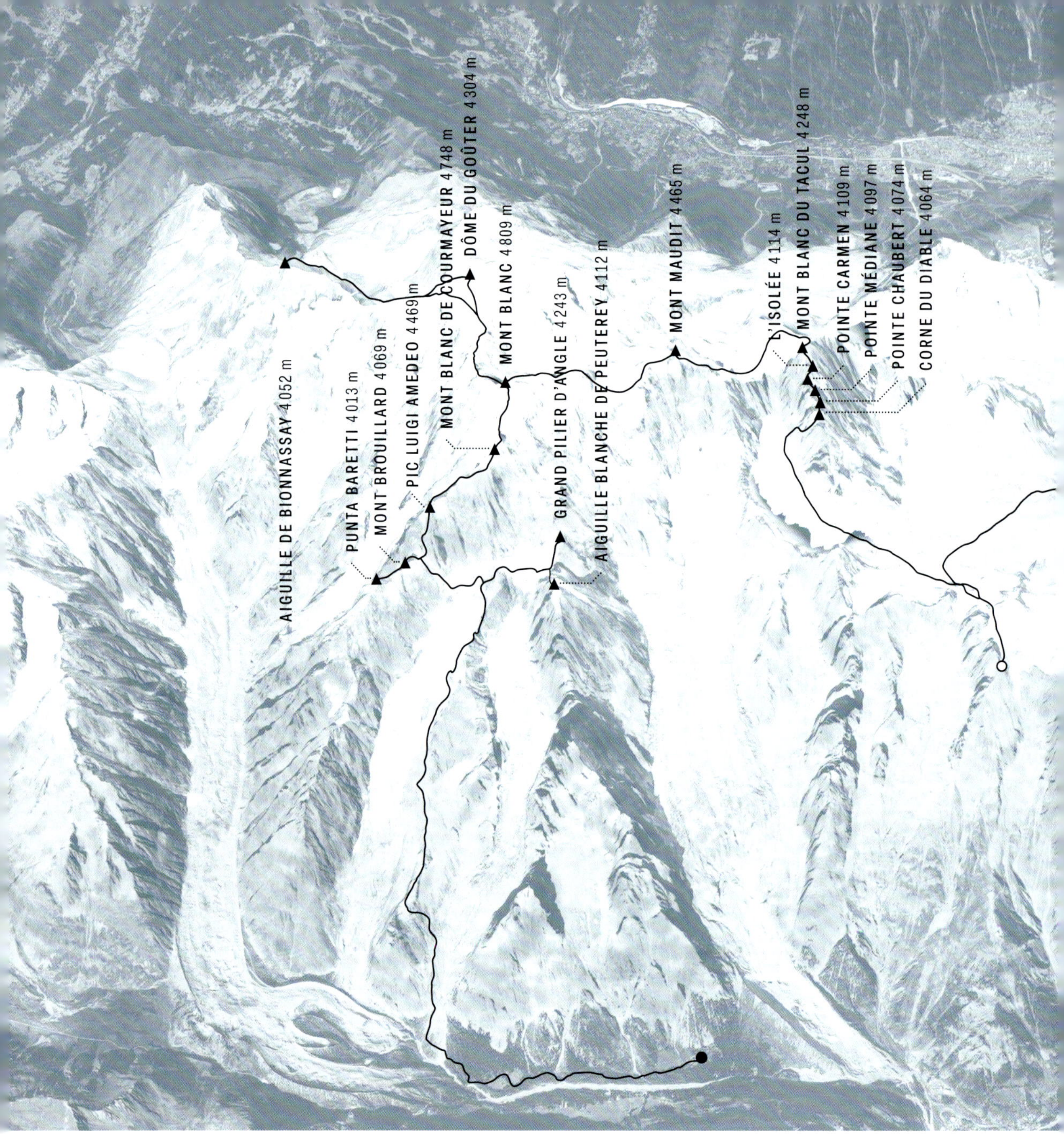

STAGES:
13–14

CLIMBING

TOTAL ELEVATION GAIN:
8,420 m/27,625 ft

TOTAL SLEEP:
14:00:00

TOTAL PEAKS > 4,000 m (13,123 ft):
20

TOTAL DISTANCE:
64.84 km (40.3 miles)

TOTAL ACTIVITY:
46:51:48

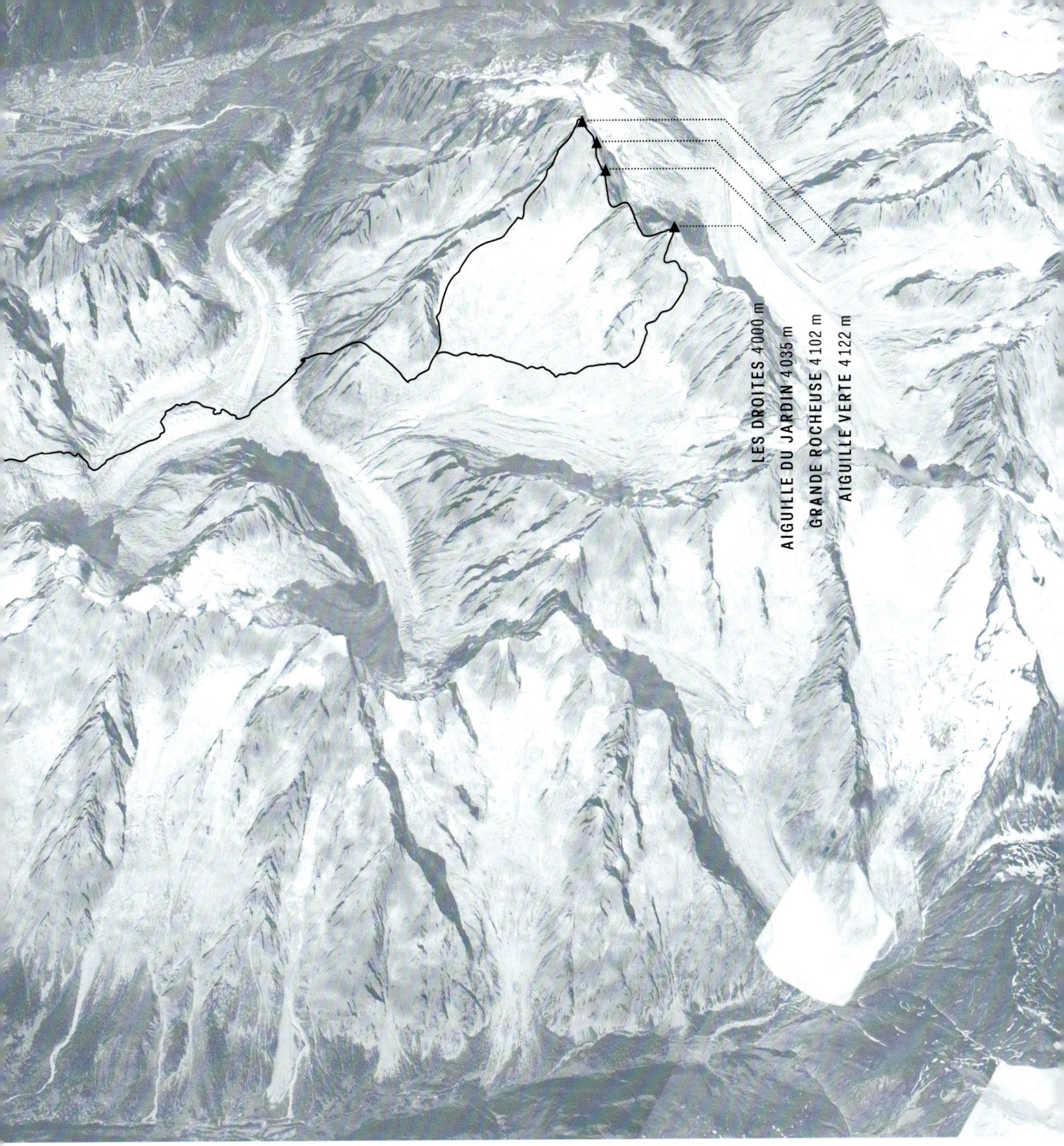
LES DROITES 4 000 m
AIGUILLE DU JARDIN 4 035 m
GRANDE ROCHEUSE 4 102 m
AIGUILLE VERTE 4 122 m

ELEVATION:

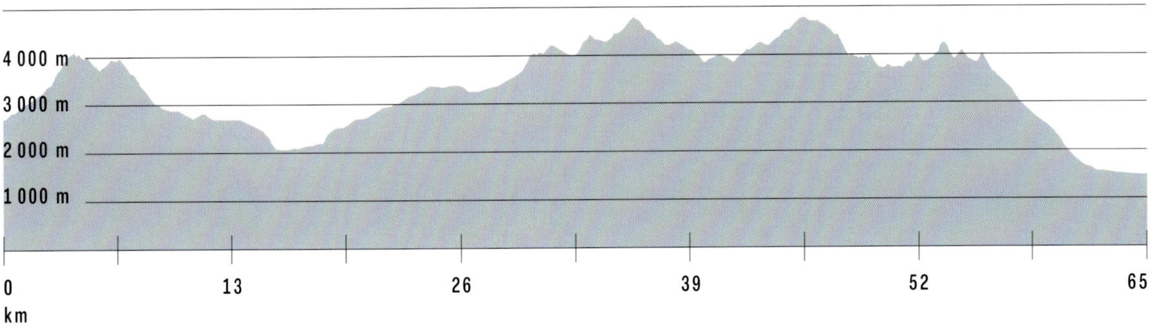
4 000 m
3 000 m
2 000 m
1 000 m
0
13
26
39
52
65
km

THE FINAL PUSH

STAGES: 15–16	80.	GRAN PARADISO	4 061 m
	81.	BARRE DES ÉCRINS	4 102 m
	82.	DÔME DE NEIGE	4 015 m

175

The last two days had arrived, and with them the final two stages that would cap off this incredible *Alpine Connections* project. Looking back, I was overcome by a sense of vertigo. I remember planning the routes, fully aware that my predictions could only be rough, and already feeling in my body and mind the ecstasy I hoped the landscapes would bring, weighing the dangers I would inevitably face, and thinking of the friends I would encounter along the way...

My goal was now within reach and there was only one final push to make. I was extremely fatigued, but I was less tired than I thought I would be. Despite everything, I felt pretty good. The body's ability to adapt to the most extreme situations and the most strenuous efforts never ceases to amaze me. It gets used to everything, and if you treat it with respect, it's unlikely to let you down. Yet you must know it well to test your own limits and progress, even under unforeseen circumstances. During the toughest stages, the connection between my body and mind had been essential for me to come out unscathed (or nearly so) from the challenges that nature had thrown at me. Looking back, there were times when I took risks that perhaps I shouldn't have, now knowing what I went through. But now wasn't the time to dwell on that. I wanted to enjoy the next two days to the fullest, in the company of my friends, and bid farewell to these mountains that fascinate me, even though I've known them for many years.

On the fifteenth day, I once again crossed the Italian border to climb the 4,061 metres (13,323 feet) of the GRAN PARADISO summit, the solitary 4,000-metre peak that dominates the natural park extending over the Vall d'Aosta and Piedmont regions.

As the sun peeked over the horizon, I mounted my bike and rode in the direction of Pont-Saint-Martin. Joining me were my friend Mathéo Jacquemoud, a companion on many adventures, and Vivian Bruchez. It was truly enjoyable to mix physical exertion with socializing, always a fun combination.

Vivian is an extremely important person in my life. He was the one who introduced me to extreme skiing over a decade ago. He was born in the Chamonix Valley, and it goes without saying that he is a key figure in the living history of the capital of mountaineering. He is an extraordinary skier, driven by a remarkable passion for the steepest slopes of the Mont Blanc massif. He learned to ski when he was three years old, and only one year later he did his first descent of the Grands Montets. His parents, sister and brother are also ski instructors. He is part of an incredible world. These mountains feel like an extension of his body. This is his home.

↑ 30.08.24/LA SORGENTE CAMPSITE
The bike was my faithful companion at the start of the penultimate stage of the project, along with Mathéo and Vivian.

← P. 174
30.08.24/GRAN PARADISO
The Gran Paradiso was less technical than the section I'd just completed, which meant a quicker ascent and descent.

→ 30.08.24/VITTORIO EMANUELE II MOUNTAIN HUT
It's a real pleasure to do the linkups with a friend by my side. With Henri Aymonod, we talked about life, work and friendship.

Halfway along the trail, we were joined by Henri Aymonod, a young and powerful mountain runner from Val di Rhêmes, and we all discussed life, work and friendships.

When we arrived, Vivian left us and returned along the same route. He had injured himself and couldn't climb, but he could still cycle. The renowned ski mountaineering champion Emily Harrop took his place. Another child of the mountains. She's only half joking when she says that she was born with two ski bindings on her feet and two poles in her hands, surrounded by the mountains that have defined her way of life. Her sport is highly demanding, and she always knows how to face the challenges that arise, aware that her greatest strength is her versatility.

Climbing up Gran Paradiso, the eightieth summit climbed so far, I was feeling pretty good. Maybe it was because I'd had sufficient sleep, which was unusual. Or perhaps it was because I had eaten well, and plenty of it. But I think that it was also because I had managed to bring mind and body into alignment after the most demanding routes of the past few days. When I say demanding, I am mainly referring to the cognitive aspects. In any case, I had managed to reach the summit quickly and easily: in just four hours. It was nothing compared with the seemingly endless hours spent, just before, on the ridges of Mont Blanc, which is extremely technically challenging. Gran Paradiso is so much easier and much less technically demanding.

We ran downhill, stopping at the Vittorio Emanuele II hut, named in 1884 to honour the former King of Italy, who was a frequent visitor to this area, which was a royal hunting ground at that time. What we'll never know is whether the monarch ever had the pleasure of savouring a *crostata* as good as the one we ate that day at the hut that still bears his name.

After this restorative break, we continued towards Pont-Saint-Martin, and the journey was also a chance to recover strength. When we got there, once again, I ate quite a lot. My body was urging me to replenish what those days of relentless activity had depleted.

Henri had to run off quickly because he had to drive to the start of a race he was running the next day. I later learned that he finished third! A great result as it is a tough race.

To continue my recovery plan, I ran along an enchanting path that leads to the Nivolet Pass in Italy, and then to the Loze Pass, back on French ground. After the second pass, I descended to Le Fornet, a traditional Alpine village in the Haute Tarentaise,

↑ 30.08.24/VITTORIO EMANUELE II MOUNTAIN HUT
It was wonderful to bring together friends and other talented people on this traverse; I have fond memories of these shared moments. The stop at the Italian hut was restorative and gave me the strength to carry on.

→ 30.08.24/VITTORIO EMANUELE II MOUNTAIN HUT
I will never forget the warmth of the people we encountered in the mountain huts.

↑ 30.08.24/LE FORNET
To end the day, I ran across the border to Val d'Isère to meet up with my team and get some serious rest: I slept for seven hours, almost an eternity for me.

← 30.08.24/GRAN PARADISO
We reached peak number 80 in just over four hours, and I was feeling great.

very close to Val d'Isère. My team were waiting for me there. I rested very deliberately, seven hours in fact – an eternity!

The following day was the sixteenth and final day: my *Petite balade alpine* was drawing to a close. An emotional day lay ahead of me in every sense. Not only because it was the culmination of the challenge I had set myself, but also because of everything I had experienced along the way. It had been the most incredible experience, one that had helped me to better understand my limits, one that I had been able to share with dear friends, some of whom I hadn't seen for a long time.

I started the final stage at the first light of dawn, leaving from Val d'Isère. I tackled a tough 172-kilometre (107-mile) bike ride, with close to 4,000 metres (13,123 feet) of ascent, to reach the Écrins National Park.

First, I climbed up the Col de l'Iseran, a pass that I knew quite well. As a child, I had spent time there cycling as well as using roller skis, during the summer training camps in Tignes with the Spanish ski mountaineering team. It was emotional being back. The landscape is stunning this side of the Alps, full of glaciers and green meadows in summer, with spectacular views.

Next, I climbed up the Col du Mont Cenis, renowned for its breathtaking lake at the top. From there, I continued on towards Susa. The heat was getting to me; it was unusually hot, even for late August. I still made it quickly to Montgenèvre, a village of fewer than 500 located right on the French-Italian border, and from there I continued towards Briançon. This city famous for both its history and artistic heritage, is the highest in France and the second highest in Europe – after Davos in Switzerland.

I felt like I was floating, almost like a cloud. I was feeling quite serene. My primary occupation, with a half-smile on my face, was to savour the final day of this amazing journey of more than 1,000 kilometres (620 miles), which had carried me physically from the eastern Alps to this point and, spiritually, to unknown places that will stay with me forever.

At Vallouise, I met up with Léo Viret, another dear friend I had the chance to catch up with during the trip. We had first met during my ski mountaineering days, and he now coaches some of the best athletes in the sport. We cycled the last stretch together, chatting about a lot of things: physiology, training methods and outlooks on life.

I arrived at Pré de Madame Carle just after four in the afternoon. I was supposed to meet up with Mathéo, who was coming from Chamonix, but he hadn't arrived yet. However, I found my mum and Aina waiting for me. I made the most it and sat with them, ate a little and we reflected on what the last two weeks had represented: the dangers, the joys, the disappointments and the emotional impact I had felt. The end was near, almost within reach, but it wasn't there yet.

Mathéo finally arrived soon after five, and we were later joined by Benjamin Védrines, one of the best mountaineers of his generation. Benjamin had in fact just returned from an expedition to K2, during which he achieved a record ascent of the world's second-highest mountain at 8,611 metres (28,251 feet). He had posted about his achievement on social media, reporting in just a few words: 'K2 in a single day without oxygen. New record: 11 hours.' My goodness, what an amazing journey, Benjamin!

We started to head up towards the Glacier Blanc. The ascent was so gentle, it felt like we were walking through a meadow. We moved at a steady pace, as we chatted about our projects, our lives – this and that.

→ 31.08.24/TRALENTA
The start of the last stage was a long bike ride to reach the Écrins.

→ PP. 184–185
31.08.24/TRALENTA
The route was beautiful and it gave me the chance to rediscover places I hadn't seen in a long time, like the Col de l'Iseran.

When we reached the glacier, we started jogging. Truth be told, it did me good to 'move around' after so many days. Twenty years ago, I ran along this glacier to achieve my first FKT, fastest known time. I used to enjoy taking on challenges like this. In trail running, this term is commonly used to describe a race with no organization and no rules. The only goal is to beat a record set by an athlete on a particular route. It's easy to see why a challenge like this is so popular. I broke the record that Jean Pellissier had set on DÔME DE NEIGE (4,015 m/13,173 ft). A decade later, Mathéo broke it. Glory is always fleeting. I was really excited to run this route with Benjamin, who's already one of the best mountaineers – skilled and fast – of his generation.

The sunset caught us at the foot of the dome, with wonderful reddish hues on the mountains to the north. This sunset seemed to carry all the sunsets of the past fifteen days, and nostalgia tightened my chest.

After the Dôme, we continued along the rocky ridge towards the BARRE DES ÉCRINS (4,102 m/13,458 ft). Once there, we celebrated our achievement with a short but meaningful embrace. We goofed around a little, they teased me about my shoes and we laughed when Benjamin randomly got a madeleine out of his rucksack. Such peace in the night...Only our words disturbed the silence. The sky felt close enough to touch.

We descended by the ridge and the glacier. We came across a couple of climbers who were camping on the glacier; they cheered for our journey and welcomed us completely naked! Mountain people are such a peculiar bunch...

On the way down, Benjamin was unlucky and twisted his ankle. Despite this misfortune, we reached Pré de Madame Carle before midnight. Aina, Núria, David, Joel, Nick and Joan were all waiting for us there. We didn't say all that much. Perhaps we didn't need to. We just rested, shared some pizzas, sitting on camping chairs, lit by our headlamps. Then we went to sleep.

That's how the *Alpine Connections* project quietly concluded. Maybe there was no better way to end it – without pomp or celebration. Words were unnecessary and life goes on. And maybe what I had achieved wasn't so important after all, even though the experience had changed me forever, in the deepest and most intense way.

Other limits, unknown to me, were waiting to be pushed beyond.

↑ 31.08.24/PRÉ DE MADAME CARLE
I got all the gear ready, then met up with Mathéo, Noa and Benjamin Védrines to take on the last two peaks of the project in the Écrins massif.

→ 31.08.24/GLACIER BLANC
We started to climb along the Glacier Blanc towards the Dôme de Neige and the Barre des Écrins; all the while we spoke about the mountains, our projects and this dream that we were so close to reaching.

→ PP. 188–191
31.08.24/GLACIER BLANC
In this final stage, I also realized how threatened glaciers are. The Écrins massif loses around 3 per cent of its mass every year.

‘There are moments, steeped in history, that one hopes to share. It took Kilian only nineteen days. But numbers alone are not enough to understand what he had accomplished. Commitment, adaptability and self-exploration are what I take away from his odyssey.’

BENJAMIN VÉDRINES

Benjamin Védrines is a mountaineer and high-mountain guide who is passionate about ski mountaineering, paragliding, climbing, cycling and cross-country skiing. His track record is filled with exceptional achievements, such the ascent of K2 without oxygen in a single day.

←↑ 31.08.24/PRÉ DE MADAME CARLE
We completed this epic traverse at midnight. The team was waiting for me. We simply shared some pizza – no pomp. A simple celebration for a major achievement.

STAGES:
15–16

BIKING
TRAIL RUNNING

TOTAL PEAKS > 4,000 m (13,123 ft):
3

TOTAL ELEVATION GAIN:
10,687 m/35,062 ft

TOTAL DISTANCE:
289.15 km/179.7 miles

TOTAL SLEEP:
14:00:00

TOTAL ACTIVITY:
24:09:32

GRAN PARADISO 4 061 m

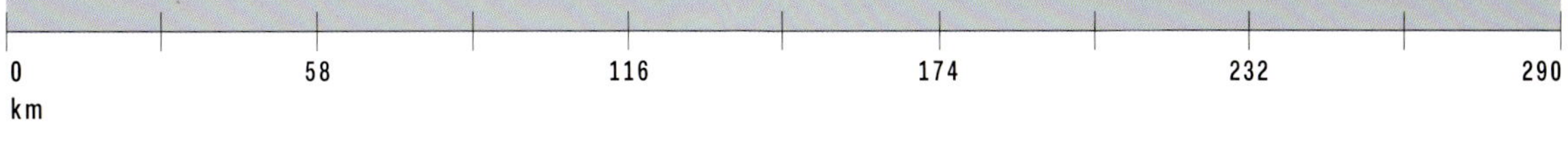
ELEVATION:
4 000 m
3 000 m
2 000 m
1 000 m
0
58
116
174
232
290
km

WHAT I LEARNED

197

Once a journey is over, we emerge changed from who we were at the outset. Yet it's not always easy to grasp the true impact of this change. Often, it's only with time that we come to understand it, when we are faced with new or unexpected challenges. On a journey like the *Alpine Connections*, a lot was stirred within me. Now I need some peace and calm to properly digest it all as any change affects mind and body alike.

What I can definitely be proud of is how I managed my physical fitness and maintained a stable weight throughout. It was one of my main concerns ahead of the journey, because during my Pyrenees crossing, my body had gradually worn down over the days. Here in the Alps, on the other hand, if I lost 2 kilos on one stage, I would easily gain them back on the easier stages. I weighed exactly the same – 54 kilos (119 pounds) – at the start in Sierre-Zinal as I did at the end of the final Écrins stage. The way my body behaved allowed me to keep a constant pace throughout the journey, even if it meant a loss of power and speed. The last two days, on Gran Paradiso and Écrins, proved that I had lost almost nothing in terms of conditioning. My hands held up well too, with minimal pain or other after-effects.

I think this is because I arrived in good shape at the start of the project, and also thanks to an appropriate fuelling strategy during the stages. I chose to stick closely to my circadian rhythm, eating infrequently but always in substantial amounts. When I was descending, in between mountains, I ate food that was easy to digest. I also stayed well hydrated between stages, because during the climbs, the only water I had was what I was carrying: a litre (34 fl oz) that would last five, six or even twenty hours, depending on the stage.

I was also fortunate to receive valuable advice from Jesús and Sergi on what nutrients – both macro and micro – to take in order to recover my strength at the end of each day. Managing my nutrition, including both calorie intake and the nutrients required for proper absorption and recovery, is a key factor.

I did most of the climbing with gloves on, so my hands didn't suffer too much. My feet fared relatively well too: I only had a few calluses on the soles of my feet and where the skin was in contact with the crampons. Whenever parts of my body hurt – like my rib or my left extensor retinaculum – it was due to injuries I had sustained.

The pain in my rib began throbbing two or three days after I fractured it, especially during opposition moves while climbing, but it eventually subsided completely. Once back at home,

← P. 196
21.08.24/ZINAL
After thirty hours in the elements, I no longer felt human. Time seemed to melt away, and my brain was in another place entirely.

however, the pain flared up suddenly, lasting a couple of weeks. This was due to the way my brain processed the nerve signals during a period when my routine required sustained activity for several hours, involving many movements that engaged the rib.

This experience helped me understand our capacity for adaptation, both hormonally and neurologically. In the short term, when faced with a fall, an avalanche or rockfall, our adrenaline kicks in and gives us a boost of energy. In the medium term, in high-risk situations where it's hard to eat properly, we are capable of maintaining a certain level of performance for hours, until we get to safety. In the long term, the body can even silence the pain of a fractured bone and allow us to continue moving for days or weeks until the end of the prolonged effort.

In the same way, it was very exciting to observe that, in situations of danger, the hormonal response can generate an increase in energy, both in intensity and duration. Specifically, we observed a release of adrenaline or cortisol in situations where I needed to keep going without sustenance, to increase my speed or to make a movement that required more strength than I thought I had in me and enter fight-or-flight mode. I am convinced that, in a traverse like this one across the Alps, the hardest part is staying alert and focused for such long periods of time, always keeping in mind that the conditions can get worse at any moment. We tend to focus heavily on physical strain, but the emotional and cognitive fatigue is even greater. I've reflected a lot about the type of effort I made on this project in comparison with previous experiences, and the biggest difference was the need to maintain full concentration the entire time.

When I finished the Pyrenees crossing, I was in a state of exhaustion, perhaps due to poor management of supplies and rest. The mental toll, however, wasn't as great because the only danger that I could foresee was a possible technical error. On this adventure, however, as the route I had planned required me to be on the ridges day and night to link the summits, the demand was higher: I needed to stay alert most of the time to face both internal dangers – such as technical errors or neuromuscular fatigue – and external ones, including crevices, rockfall and rockslides.

Traversing between mountains is nothing new; it's been done since the early days of mountaineering. But due to the evolution of equipment, technical skills and physical capabilities, as well as advances in knowledge of strategy and logistics, the potential to undertake longer or quicker traverses has grown. I am reminded of Ueli Steck, who used his paraglider to descend a few summits during his traverse, or how, in 2024, the paragliding mountaineers Peter von Känel and Chrigel Maurer traversed the eighty-two four-thousanders in fifty-one days, using paragliders not only to descend from the summits, but also to travel the great distances in between ridges.

The fact that I was able to climb the Alps' four-thousanders in just nineteen days – a much shorter time than on previous traverses – wasn't primarily because of improved physical abilities but rather the different strategy we carefully designed and put into practice.

Looking at past link-ups, we find that shorter ones, ranging from a few hours to two or three days, were completed without sleep or with only minimal rest. On the longer link-ups, however, the strategy was to link up a few summits during the day, then descend to get some rest – day after day.

For this *Alpine Connections* challenge, the first objective I set myself was to reconcile these two approaches; that is, to apply a non-stop style to a long connection. From a physical perspective, the unknown was how long the body can be pushed before it needs to rest, how long the rest should last and how to manage energy intake so it can be truly restorative.

Another unknown was how to deal with weather conditions. When undertaking a short link-up, you try to find a good weather window and set off when conditions are at their best. So it's reasonable to think that you can plan to do certain sections of the route when the conditions are optimum, whether it's the temperature, rock stability or snow hardness. When completing a long link-up in a single push, it's impossible to predict the weather over such a long period and plan ideal windows for safe progress.

Through *Alpine Connections*, I learned that the key to success in a long-term venture is knowing how to manage bad weather and challenging conditions. Above all, it requires having plenty of leeway to improvise, because there are many factors that cannot be controlled and danger can appear from anywhere. This proved a real challenge for the logistics team: coordinating every detail without knowing when I would reach the hut or, for the cameras, how long we would remain at the summit above 4,000 metres. You need to acquire a lot of technical and strategic knowledge to stay safe and protected when the situation becomes difficult. Above all, it is essential to have extremely strong emotional control to cope with the stress generated by these high-stakes situations.

→ 21.08.24 / ZINAL
Alpine Connections was also a journey of self-discovery: listening to my body, knowing when to rest, understanding my physical condition and being able to draw conclusions from the physiological data.

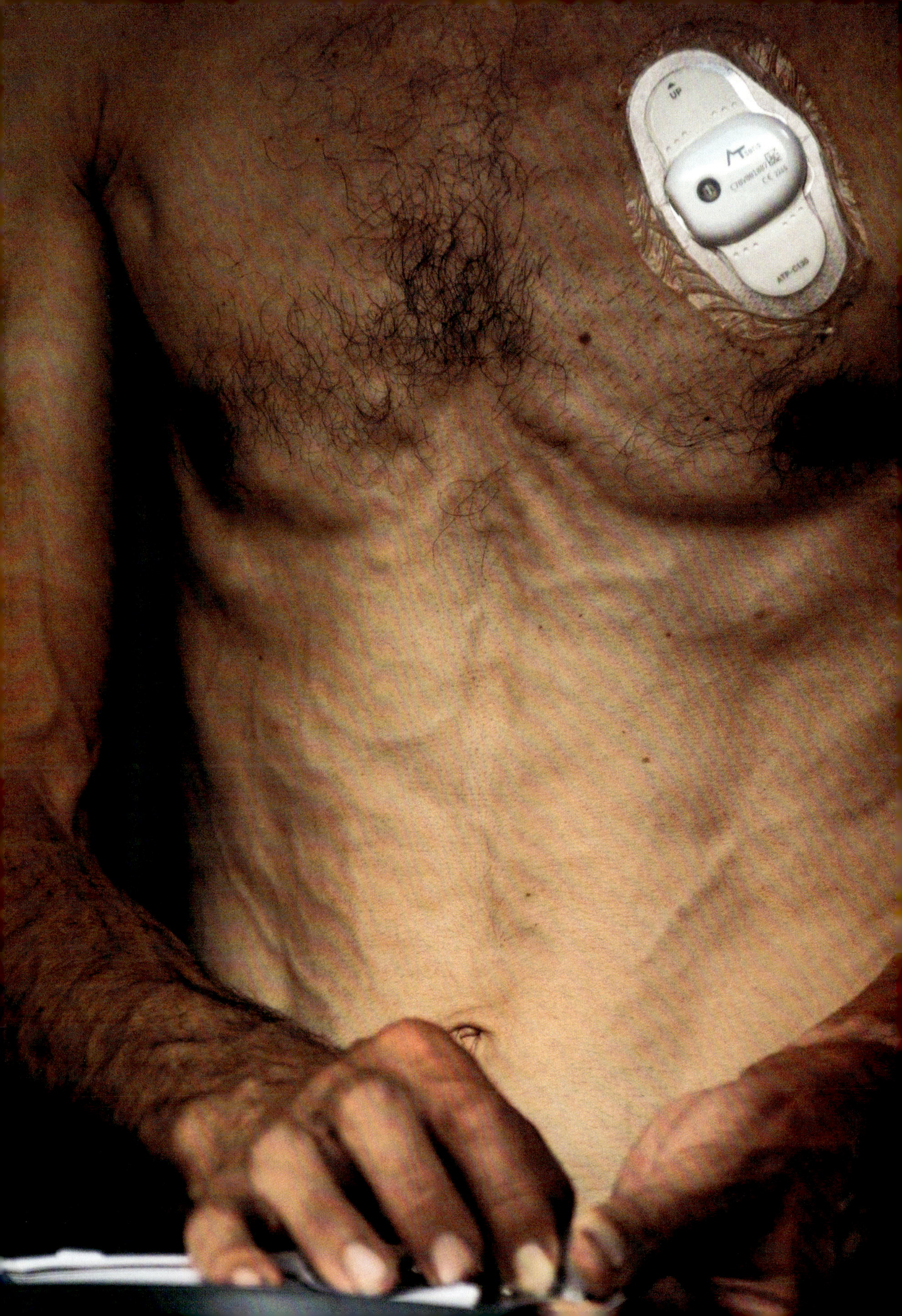
UP

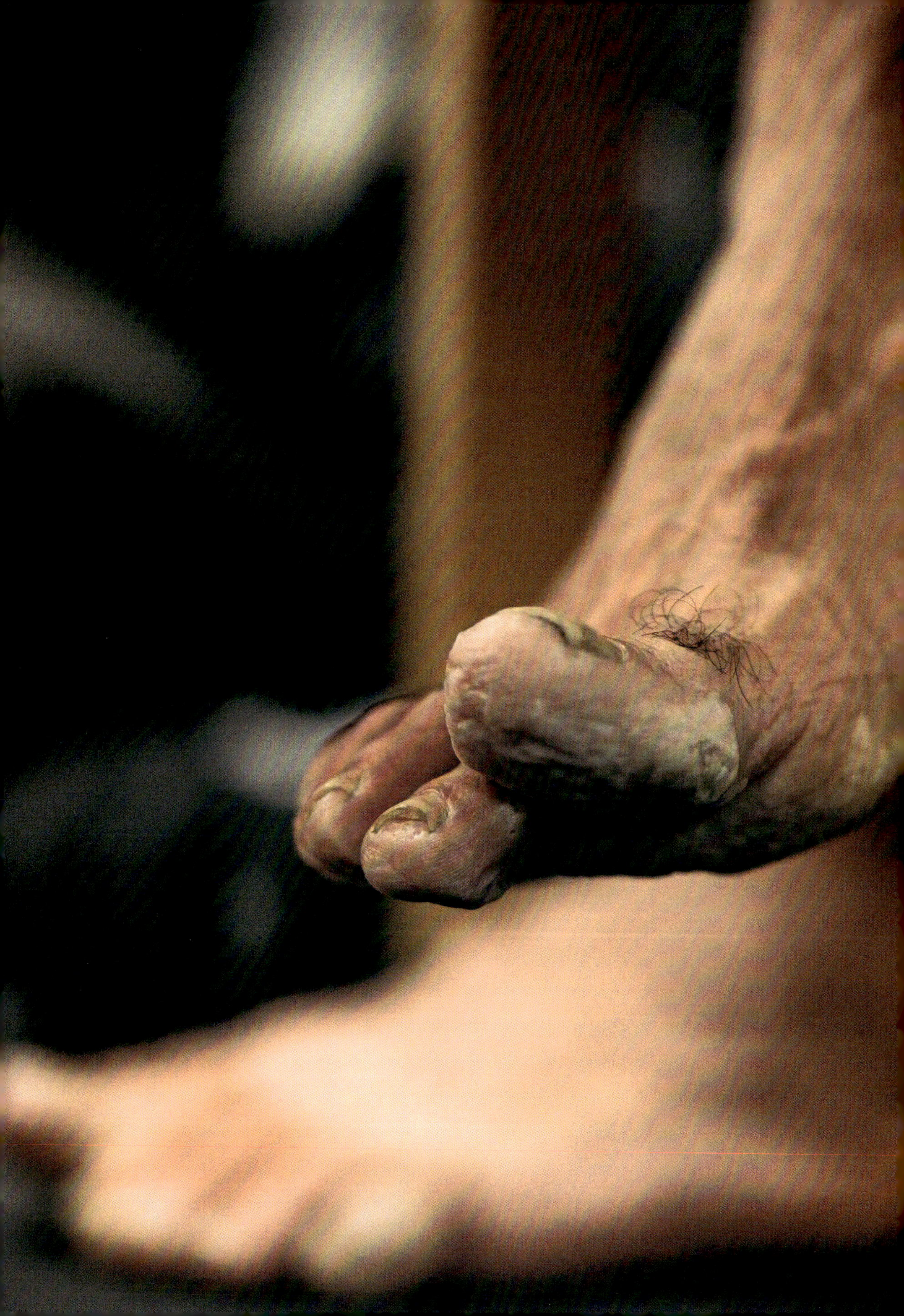

← **21.08.24 / HÖRNLI MOUNTAIN HUT**
Strain, exhaustion and stress were ever present throughout this adventure. The key factor was mental and physical control, in addition to allowing time for recovery.

And that was exactly my primary concern: how to remain fully focused and concentrated while I was engaging in very stressful activities for such long stretches of time. Adding to the challenge is the fatigue and sleep deprivation that accumulate over consecutive days, each harder than the one before.

In such endeavours, two factors come into play and complement each other. The first is the experience gained from previous undertakings involving a great deal of stress, especially over a long period of time, such as climbing solo, on loose rock and in terrible weather conditions, for example. In these situations, when confronted with danger, it doesn't take much effort to make a decision; it's almost automatic in fact, thanks to gained experience. The second factor depends on each person's temperament. It is particularly important, as a person's character determines whether they can regain their composure and return to a state of complete relaxation after facing such stressful situations – thereby minimizing mental strain and energy drain.

With all this in mind, I am reminded of a story that left a strong impression on me during my first experience in the Himalayas. I was in a hostel having tea while, outside, winter kept piling more and more snow on the mountains we wanted to climb. I listened carefully to my two companions, both extensively experienced in technical, high-altitude mountaineering. Out of the blue, Jordi Corominas started thinking about the purpose of what we were doing, and he shared an idea that has stuck with me to this day:

'You only truly understand mountaineering the day you get home and find yourself completely unable to describe what you've done.'

And to emphasize his point, he added: 'Have I been climbing? Yes, but that's not what's made it so special...Have I been sleeping outside in the snow? Yes, but it's not about that...Have I been walking on treacherous terrain and am I physically exhausted? Yes, but there's more to it...'

Perhaps – and this is just a thought – this is the essence of mountaineering: putting to use the tools and knowledge we've acquired over years to tackle the various challenges the mountain throws at us.

In this *Alpine Connections* project, upon closer inspection, the numbers don't matter all that much. It's true that the most technically challenging section of the traverse posed a certain level of difficulty, but it's known for its stable rock and it's also a standard route, so navigation didn't play a role. Other routes

‘You only truly understand mountaineering the day you get home and find yourself completely unable to describe what you’ve done.’

JORDI COROMINAS

Jordi Corominas is a Catalan mountaineer and high-mountain guide. Winner of the Piolet d’Or (‘Golden Ice Axe’), Jordi is famous for being the first person to complete the first and second solo ascents of the Magic Line on K2 without supplemental oxygen.

Normal
Norma

of a lower grade seemed much more technical than expected, while some, attempted in the middle of a snowstorm, became far more complicated.

On this adventure, I didn't open any new route, nor did I face any particularly difficult climb. That said, words fail me to express its true depth. This is perhaps what lies at the heart of its beauty: having experienced the journey as it is, without the need to define it, and accepting that some experiences can only be felt, not explained.

No metrics or labels can fully capture the deeply personal emotions this meaningful project has stirred within me. Even today, they continue to drive me from within, urging me to seek new horizons where I can reconnect with my body, nature, and the mountains I hold so dear. For in the end, it is not about conquest, but about continuing onward with a heart wide open.

→ 20.08.24 / VALAIS
The *Alpine Connections* changed me. At times, I didn't know if I was awake or in a dream. It will take me some time to come down from these mountains.

WE MUST ACT NOW

‘I have climbed mountains and crossed glaciers all my life, and I was able to observe the devastating effects of climate change. During the *Alpine Connections* project, I explored the limits of human capability. As I pushed those boundaries, I also witnessed firsthand the environment reaching its own limits. The permafrost is thawing, which poses a major risk to the mountains. It is one of the most significant climate factors I have witnessed, and it represents a threat to all. What is alarming is the speed at which these changes are taking place. The beauty and significance of the ecosystems I traversed are remarkable, and protecting them has become a vital necessity.’

KILIAN JORNET

HUMAN IMPACT ON THE MOUNTAINS

Globally, mountain ranges provide essential water resources for nearly half of the world’s population. The Alps are no exception: a vital and fragile ecosystem on which a large part of the European population depends. Approximately fourteen million people live in the Alps, spread across over six thousand communities in eight countries. By combining agricultural traditions with tourism, they help to preserve the area’s unique natural and cultural heritage.

Yet, human influence is transforming this environment. Urban expansion in valleys and towns, air pollution from transport, industry and tourism, and extensive infrastructure development all contribute to the degradation of our mountains. To make matters worse, global warming and the albedo effect, i.e. the loss of reflective surfaces such as ice and snow, could drive temperature increases in the Alpine regions of around 1.5 °C by the mid-21st century.

Mountains and glaciers play a crucial role in maintaining the natural balance, from the water cycle and permafrost to biodiversity. The Kilian Jornet Foundation is working to preserve these environments for future generations to enjoy, in the broader context of a healthier planet. For this reason, from the beginning, we were by Kilian’s side during one of the most significant adventures of his sporting journey, not only in terms of the physical demands, but also for everything it represented. Being by his side on this journey meant much more than walking in his footsteps: it was an immersion in the beauty of the Alps and a firsthand awareness of their fragility.

PERMAFROST: THE INVISIBLE GLUE OF THE MOUNTAINS

> 'Global warming is causing mountains to age more quickly, weakening their resilience and softening their distinctive shapes.'
>
> DR FLORENCE MAGNIN
> Researcher at EDyTEM
> (Mountain Environments, Dynamics and Territories)

Above an altitude of 2,500 metres (8,202 feet), much of what keeps mountains stable depends on permafrost, a layer of soil frozen permanently, which maintains the cohesion of the terrain. Indeed, it covers an area three times larger than that of the glaciers. But this 'natural glue' is melting at a fast pace, causing landslides, rockfall and notable changes in mountain morphology.

Kilian witnessed firsthand the thawing of permafrost in various sections of the route. In the Bernina Massif, only a few months before Kilian's passage, there was a massive landslide at the Piz Scerscen. The frequency of these events is increasing, and they may cause chain reactions. In May 2025, a landslide probably caused by unstable permafrost initiated the collapse of the Birch Glacier in the Lötschental Valley. This disaster led to devastating consequences: it partially destroyed the village of Blatten and blocked the Lonza River.

For this reason, it is essential to monitor and assess the impact of climate change on the permafrost, in particular to identify associated risks, such as terrain instability and landslides, so that we can act in time.

GLACIERS: VISIBLE SENTINELS OF CLIMATE CHANGE

> 'All is not lost, we still have one last chance to preserve the majority of the world's glacier ice and safeguard glaciers and post-glacial ecosystems, but we need policymakers to take action.'
>
> JEAN-BAPTISTE BOSSON
> Glaciologist at Marge Sauvage and coordinator of Ice&Life

Glaciers probably bear the most visible evidence of climate change. During his challenge, Kilian observed the changes these ecosystems have undergone since the beginning of his sporting career. Their accelerated retreat not only impacts fresh water supply, but also biodiversity, geomorphology and the surrounding ecosystems. On a global scale, glaciers – excluding the two large ice sheets in Antarctica and Greenland – have lost 5 per cent of their volume since 2000 but, in mountainous regions like the French Alps, they have lost 70 per cent of their surface area since 1850.

A recent example of this fragility occurred in La Bérarde, in the Écrins, just a few weeks before Kilian finished his journey there: heavy rainfall and sudden thaw caused the Étançons torrent to overflow, destroying the eponymous town, one of the birthplaces of French mountaineering. It is believed that the retreat of the Glacier de Bonne Pierre may have led to the creation of a lake that ended up overflowing.

To protect these ice giants and preserve these vital ecosystems, we need to cut greenhouse gas emissions, include glaciers in national park conservation plans and strengthen preservation efforts.

BIODIVERSITY IN THE ALPS: A TREASURE THAT MUST BE PROTECTED

> 'When we realize that we are not separate from nature, but an integral part of it, our sense of responsibility towards the environment naturally deepens.'
>
> JÉRÉMIE VILLET
> Wildlife photographer

Another remarkable aspect of the traverse was how it brought to light the Alps' extraordinary biodiversity: more than 30,000 animal and 13,000 plant species perfectly adapted to extreme conditions. But this fragile balance is under threat. Scientists from CREA Mont-Blanc, specialists in Alpine biodiversity, have observed that, as temperatures increase, many species move to higher altitudes to find suitable living conditions, but they are often left without a habitat. According to the International Union for Conservation of Nature (IUCN) Red List, nearly 30 per cent of the 169,000 species assessed worldwide are threatened with extinction – a warning sign of the global biodiversity crisis that sadly also affects Alpine ecosystems.

The Alps are a sanctuary for wildlife, and preserving a high level of biodiversity is fundamental to the health and stability of the ecosystem. Alpine forests are essential allies against climate change, capable of absorbing up to 30 per cent of human-induced CO_2 emissions in the region. They also provide protection against avalanches and help retain water. However, this rich natural heritage is under significant threat due to climate change and human activities.

In response to these issues, as part of the *Alpine Connections* project we wanted to highlight efforts in sustainable development, clean transport, emissions reduction and responsible consumption.

THE KILIAN JORNET FOUNDATION'S ROLE IN THE *ALPINE CONNECTIONS* PROJECT

The Foundation embraced the challenge of documenting the natural significance of these landscapes and the threats they face, bringing attention and visibility to all that often goes unnoticed on the Alpine summits. This was a unique opportunity to raise public awareness of the current condition of this environment and highlight the effects of climate change, which are already evident.

To achieve this, we first established a network of contacts that would grant us insight into the life of this environment: scientists, local figures, athletes and other engaged citizens who helped us understand the condition of every corner of the natural environment Kilian passed through. To combine their voices and efforts, we decided to build an interactive map of the traverse, which soon became a dynamic tool offering a wide range of contributions. Our goals were clear: to study and make known the present conditions and factual information about glaciers, biodiversity, permafrost and the global warming affecting the Alps.

This map is made up of different layers that provide a complete overview of the region. One layer covers Kilian's route and extraordinary journey. Another provides information on the current extent of glaciers, protected wildlife areas, forest reserves and the probable distribution of permafrost. You can also find a list of projects promoted by the Foundation as well as other organizations involved in conservation efforts in the region.

Raising awareness of these initiatives helps reinforce an important idea: the better we understand the natural environment, the stronger our commitment to protect it.

We deeply believe in the power of collective effort, and as such, this map is not just a compilation of information but also a meeting place among people, projects and regions united by a common goal: to protect what we love most.

CALL TO ACTION

The *Alpine Connections* project was unquestionably a unique sporting adventure, undertaken by Kilian, but it is also a commitment to the planet: to showcase the beauty of our mountains, enjoy them and rally support to protect them.

We are at a key juncture. The climate crisis is no longer a distant threat – this project makes that clear. While Killian was running, we all saw firsthand the changes taking place in the mountains. This is a unique opportunity to showcase these ecosystems and strengthen the call to cut CO_2 emissions in order to protect them.

This responsibility cannot fall solely on individual initiative. We need collective action: governments, institutions and companies need to take accountability and make brave decisions that support a sustainable future. That said, on an individual scale, each of us can adopt more sustainable habits, ultimately rethinking how we travel, eat, consume and engage in sports.

Now is the time to act. Only with decisive collective action can we protect the mountains and the planet. This is the mission of the Foundation, driven by the *Alpine Connections* project: raising awareness, understanding and protecting essential ecosystems that connect us to nature and ourselves.

INDEX

Page numbers in *italics* refer to illustrations

Kilian Jornet is a Catalan professional trail runner and ski mountaineer, widely considered among the greatest all-round mountain athletes in the world. Jornet is author of *Above the Clouds* and *Run or Die*, which have sold over 100,000 copies and been translated into fifteen languages. He also owns his own gear brand, Nnormal, and has established an environmental foundation.

Translated from the Catalan *Alps, més enllà dels límits* by Daniel Parsons

First published in the United Kingdom in 2026 by
Thames & Hudson Ltd, 6–24 Britannia Street, London WC1X 9JD

First published in the United States of America in 2026 by
Thames & Hudson Inc., 500 Fifth Avenue, New York, New York 10110

Art direction and layout: NAPO PEOPLE, Régis Tosetti & Simon Palmieri with Ernesto Luna
Photographs: David Ariño, Joel Badia, Noa Barrau and Nick Danielson

This book was translated with the help of a grant from the Institut Ramon Llull

EU Authorized Representative: Interart S.A.R.L.
19 rue Charles Auray, 93500 Pantin, Paris, France
productsafety@thameshudson.co.uk
interart.fr

A CIP catalogue record for this book is available from the British Library

Library of Congress Control Number 2026940444

ISBN 978-0-500-03203-9
01

Printed and bound in China by C&C Offset Printing Co. Ltd

MIX
Paper | Supporting responsible forestry
FSC www.fsc.org FSC® C008047

STAGES	DATE (2024)	ACTIVITY	DISTANCE (km)	ELEVATION (m)	PEAKS (+4000 m)	ACTIVITY (time)	SLEEP
1	13.08	CLIMBING	29.12	2573	1	06:42:47	
		BIKING	213.06	3984		08:55:34	4:00:00
2	14.08	CLIMBING	37.25	4496	3	17:06:08	3:30:00
3	15.08	CLIMBING	99.04	7890	0	32:30:38	
	16.08	BIKING	46.26	888	6	02:12:02	3:15:00
4	17.08	CLIMBING	30.26	3381	0	08:10:23	
		BIKING	5.22	260	2	00:22:04	7:00:00
5	18.08	CLIMBING	23.75	3246	4	08:41:35	7:00:00
6	19.08	CLIMBING	47.70	6139	7	21:27:18	6:00:00
7	20.08	CLIMBING	46.47	4907	18	17:45:29	3:00:00
8	21.08	CLIMBING	30.80	4142	3	18:08:06	4:00:00
9	22.08	CLIMBING	36.80	4297	4	18:31:50	2:00:00
10	23.08	BIKING	109.99	1490	0	04:40:00	
		CLIMBING	24.02	2786	3	09:20:55	4:00:00
11	24.08	BIKING	29.38	728	0	01:20:02	
		TRAIL	15.57	831	0	02:26:31	4:00:00
REST DAY							9:00:00
12	26.08	CLIMBING	28.29	4199	8	18:22:34	5:00:00
13	27.08	CLIMBING	24.03	3470	4	17:26:20	5:00:00
14	28.08	CLIMBING	27.01	3977	14	20:09:53	5:00:00
	29.08	CLIMBING	13.80	973	2	09:15:35	4:00:00
15	30.08	BIKING	54.63	1298	0	02:34:08	
		CLIMBING	17.45	2019	0	04:01:47	
		TRAIL	20.40	1250	1	03:28:40	7:00:00
16	31.08	BIKING	172.10	3834	0	07:53:52	
		CLIMBING	24.57	2286	2	06:11:05	7:00:00
TOTAL			1206.97	75344	82	267:45:16	*5:16:46

*AVERAGE HOURS OF SLEEP

TOTAL STATISTICS

Alpine Connections

PEAKS > 4000 m:	DAYS:	DISTANCE (km):
82	19	1206.97

View from the Écrins at the end of the adventure.